My Various Nature Experiences

BY JOHN T. ROGERS

DORRANCE PUBLISHING CO
EST. 1920
PITTSBURGH, PENNSYLVANIA 15238

Dorrance Publishing Co
585 Alpha Drive
Pittsburgh, PA 15238
Visit our website at *www.dorrancebookstore.com*

ISBN: 979-8-8868-3133-7
eISBN: 979-8-8868-3992-0

PROSPECTUS

The following stories of my attraction and efforts to mingle with Mother Nature are real. I have enjoyed watching and taking part in the workings of Mother Nature. The flora and fauna of nature create the background for so many situations that can be shown as if a naturalist had written a best seller. Over the years, I have had the pleasure of seeing many episodes of how nature continues to furnish memorable scenes and action-packed happenings as if I was part of a theatrical troop playing on the stage of life.

The reading of these stories will enable the reader to witness and enjoy how I or anyone raised in north central Wyoming can have several meaningful situations take place in Mother Nature, land where animals can still be themselves in a public or wilderness environment. It is true that I sought out the exciting natural world through my activities as a young boy or as an adult participating in Mother Nature's playground.

Big city dwellers can be part of the outdoor experiences that I have been so lucky to be a part of. I would hope that these stories will create a want in people to see and hope that they too could take part in nature by visiting our parks, wetlands, and wilderness areas. May the tourist find his/her travels exciting and fun as they partake in Mother Nature's land filled with fond memories, experiences waiting to happen. People who live or have lived in the less populated areas of the world have had experiences of their own with the animals and plants that make up their habitat. My experiences will help bring out the memories of days gone by and remind the reader of their own memories of past events that have become part of their positive or negative existence with the world of nature.

I am honored to share my experiences with the reader. Of course, I have had numerous other experiences with nature through my hunting, fishing, and traveling endeavors. I feel fortunate to have lived in the small-town environments that afforded me the chance to enjoy nature and what she has to offer. Now that I am retired from teaching (thirty-seven years) and from the National Guard (twenty-one years), I still reach out to Mother Nature through my hobbies of prospecting, fishing or traveling the back roads of Wyoming in search of nature's beauty.

My Various
Nature Experiences

BEAVERS

Throughout the years, I have had many encounters with beavers as I was fishing or just nature walking and watching. Beavers seemed always very calm and nonthreatening whenever I had contact with them. Maybe they were too busy being busy.

My first experience with a beaver was when I was about six years old. I was wandering down by a small stream behind my aunt's house (unknown to her). It was a nice warm summer day and I was getting house phobic, so I left the back yard and meandered down to the row of willows, cattails, and high grass that bordered the creek.

I found a neat little pathway through the taller-than-me flora and followed the game trail to the water. Just as I got a good look at the creek, out of the corner of my eye, I saw this huge monster standing up on the creek bank gnawing on a small twig.

Being a tough young lad, I stared at the beaver and he looked back at me as if to say, "Go away kid, you're bothering me."

Well, it did not take me long to get the message. I turned around and ran back up the trail and to the house. After reaching the back porch, I stuttered my extreme fright to my aunt.

My aunt, to my surprise, was not even a little bit scared as she heard me explain the hazardous venture. In fact, she started laughing and asked me if a chocolate chip cookie would calm my nerves. All I could say was, "Sure." She led me into the kitchen and produced a nice warm cookie. While I was washing down a couple cookies with milk, my aunt lectured me on the animal called a beaver and the role they play in Mother Nature land. From that time on, I have always enjoyed observing beavers at work in the wild. But I did have to take some teasing from my siblings and adults about my first encounter with the majestic beaver.

Later in my life, we moved to an ideal place for a kid to be raised. Well, it was for me. I was always a loner and could entertain myself quite easily. We lived four miles out of a small town (Byron) in north central Wyoming. We lived on a farm/ranch located between a temperate desert to the southeast and a creek and river bottom to the northwest. The difference in scenery was amazing. I had chores to do, but also had plenty of time to wander and explore all the surrounding regions. It was a time in my life that I look back on with many smiles and much wonderment. The days of Tom Sawyer and Huck Finn had nothing over me.

We had an old barn that had lived out an old life and was seldom used except by the pigeons. I built a fort in the rafters. This served two main purposes. The first was to have a place to hide out and dream of those things that young boys dream of. I also could watch the lifespan of pigeons from the egg to the adult. This was exciting to me. Eventually a new blacktop highway was going to be built and we had to demolish the building. It was a sad time. The road also took away the sandy region which my friend and I build a wonderful dugout with tunnels between rooms. We hauled out a lot of dirt with buckets and rope. At that time, I felt as I'm sure the Indians felt. I was not in favor of progress.

Not to be a couch potato, I built my new fort in the rafters of the granary. It served as a sanctuary for me to get away and dream and again the pigeons were present to entertain me. The creek bottom which laid across the highway was so inviting with its different flora and fauna. Me and Daniel Bone had a lot of area to explore. There were a lot of game trails (some cow) to follow. Many forts to make and animals to identify and observe. This small creek (Whistle Creek) was a tributary to the Shoshoni River. The mouth of Whistle Creek was only a couple miles off. I called both watersheds my domain. It was here and the desert that allowed me tremendous adventures with the wildlife that frequented the region.

Well, getting back to the beaver. The fields around the area are elevated over the two watersheds. This allows a young boy to lay down on the edge of the hill on a nice warm summer day and look down at the agenda of different animals as they go about their daily routines. It so happens that the field irrigation water ends up running through a pipe that sticks out from the side of the hill (stopping much erosion of the hillside). From this water, a series of three beaver ponds were formed. What a stage for the birds and animals to play on. It was a pleasure to be part of the audience. I spent many a day observing and collecting in my mind the enjoyable sights I saw from each scene Mother Nature produced.

Sometimes the river would flood its flood plain and extra water would end up running through the beaver ponds. This would cause the beaver dams to partially wash out and the beavers had to work overtime to get their dams back to working order. It was a learning environment as I watched them cut drag and repair their dams.

Most of my adventures with beavers came in my middle age years as I was fishing on the Wind River/Big Horn River. The river is called the Wind River from its source in Yellowstone Park until it goes through the Wind River Canyon until it arrives at a spot called "the wedding of the waters". Then the river is called the Big Horn River until it runs into the Yellowstone River in Montana.

One day I was going to fish a backwater area in the Big Horn River. I have caught and released some nice rainbow and brown trout from the area. Just traveling on the roads to get there creates wandering thoughts in my head. I drive down highway twenty south, turn right on to Black Mountain Road, then turn left on to Skeleton Road, and drive to the region where the river lets a sliver of water run around a very small island and then that water travels back to the main river over a wide area of cobble rock, forming shallow rapids. Where the waters meet, a nice back-whirl is created. The fish like to wait in the slower water for bits of food to float down the rapids or for the minnows living in the back-whirl itself.

After pulling over and stopping the pickup, I readied my gear for an entertaining fishing experience. I walked over to the edge of the small hillside. In order to get down to the river, I had to step down over the side of the hill and walk through some high grass and cattails to get to the water. This was no biggy. I had played this song and dance many times to get to a fishing hole. I eased myself down over the dirt side of the hill and took a long step into the vegetation. At that time, my foot moved off from under me and I found myself on my backside.

A large beaver turned and looked at me as to say, "You clumsy human animal! Why can't you watch where you are going?"

The beaver was not aggressive. In fact, his attitude reminded me of a sloth as he gave me the evil eye and waddled off down the bank and eased himself into the water. All I could do was let out a sigh and laugh.

As he headed down stream, I yelled to him, "And you have a good day."

I'm sure he did as he related the story of the strange clumsy human to his friends. Well, he was not the only one with a story to tell. Wait until I inform my friends of my beaver encounter and of course about how all the big fish got away.

On another occasion, I was wading along the edge of the river next to a high cliff bank. The shore line was quite deep sloped and a little wet. This made it tough to walk on without slipping and falling into the river. I decided to skip the falling part and just wade along the edge of the water and cast my line out into the slower moving rapids and reel the line back in up through the calmer water along the edge of the rapids. This was a proven positive tactic over the years in this area.

Today was no different. I had landed several nice rainbow trout with a four-pound brown trout thrown in for my enjoyment. As I moved along the shoreline, I came to a spot of deeper water. The river bottom seemed to be less rocky and quite smooth. It looked like there was a washed-out tunnel like area under the bank. Too busy with images of fish dangling from my pole, I just stood in front of the dug-out region and continued my routine of casting out for those fish that were waiting to make my day.

As I was enjoying reeling in another nice fish, something was brushing my inner legs. I was monetarily startled as I felt the contact. I looked down and what did I see, but two nice full-sized beavers swimming out from under the bank. They scooted right between my legs and headed down the river. I thought I saw one wink at me as it went through my legs. I wonder how many times they had played their little game with other fisherman. I can imagine their giggles as they went about their daily activities. Well, that day I had a beaver encounter and the big fish didn't get away.

On another day in the same area, except on the opposite side of the river, I was walking along the deep sloped bank. The walking was touchy as no trail existed. I had to carefully balance myself by leaning against the slope with one hand. Sometimes there was some weeds or a downed tree that I could grasp to pull myself along the hillside. While I was standing on this rather well-used beaver slide reeling in a nice rainbow trout, I was clipped from behind by some falling object and my legs buckled and I slid the thirty feet down the dirt trail into the water below. As I stood up totally wet from my ordeal, I saw this beaver off to my left. I swear he was laughing and was proud of his funny endeavor. I guess that is what I get for standing on his branch-getting runway. I just looked at him and smiled back. Again, a beaver had gotten the best of me.

Several times over the years, I have had beavers swim up to where I was fishing or lazily sitting on the bank of a stream. They would announce their presence by pounding their tail on the water to let me know that they were not pleased by my entrance in to their domain. But once they got used to the idea I was there to stay, even if it was for a little while, they went back to their busy schedule. Or were they off somewhere planning their next funny on any human fisherman that may invade their habitat. They sure have entertained me over the years. As I'm sure they have gotten many laughs at my expense.

WHITE WATER MISHAP

It sounded like a good idea to me. My brother-in-law suggested that we take my six-man rubber raft down the Wind River. The river runs through a scenic canyon south of Thermopolis, Wyoming. There are some very nice rapids located in the canyon. This was when I was younger, inexperienced, and dumber.

The canyon is a fun spot for local residence as well as those tourists traveling through the area on their way to Yellowstone Park. It provides good fishing (a tribal permit is needed). Rafting trips can be purchased by guides out of Thermopolis. Thermopolis also has the world's largest hot spring, hot water mineral swimming pools, buffalo ranch, and of course good fishing in the Wind River or Big Horn River. The river changes its name just south of Thermopolis.

It was summer time and the weather was great. My wife, her brother, his two boys, and a lady friend of the family all set out to have a good time. My brother-in-law suggested we take a small motor to attach to the raft to help push the raft along in calm water or maybe to move back upstream if we wanted to. We had two oars and life jackets.

The river was running at a good level as they were letting plenty of water out of the dam for the farmers to have irrigation water. We put in just before the three tunnels at the south entrance of the canyon. We had a couple of vehicles so we left one at the area we wanted to get out and carried the raft with my pickup. We carried the raft down the rocky incline from the highway, attached the motor, and eased the raft into the water. The lady friend sat in the bottom of the raft as she was not a good swimmer. A couple of us rode on the sides of the raft so we could use the oars to maneuver the raft through rocks that might be sticking up above the water.

I handled one oar and Charles, my brother-in-law, used the other oar as we started down the river. We did not start the motor. The six of us were in good spirits as the river current moved us along on downstream. We were hoping to see some mountain sheep that frequented the canyon or some bald eagles. We knew that that ducks and Canadian geese used this canyon.

We got to some whitewater rapids and we were braced for a good roller-coasting ride. However, the motor prop hit a submerged boulder and flipped up from the back of the raft and tore out the bottom of the raft. At the same time, one of the oars dropped through the bottom. Two passengers were hanging with their feet in the river. I tried to paddle as hard as I could to get the raft headed towards the river bank. Not far ahead, the roughest rapids in the canyon awaited us. Of course, panic was setting in by all. I continued to work as hard as I could to get the raft closer to shore. The legs of the people were being struck by submerged rocks in the river. This caused even more emphasis upon getting the raft beached on the bank. I was winning the battle of turning the raft towards the bank. Eventually the raft emerged into a slow back-whirl and floated to the river bank. Charles had long legs and was able to step into the water and help slide the raft to the shore. Then it was time to unload everyone and what supplies was left. I'm glad we had life jackets on to help those sitting on the bottom of the raft to float on the water. My arms were yelling at me for being overworked. I was just glad we were able get everyone out of the river with no serious injuries, except for our pride and the want of a fun rafting trip. My wife got a ride to my pickup. It was good to see her coming towards us. We loaded the raft and we all ended up in the city park for a picnic and an enthusiastic conversation of the float trip.

Years later, I floated the river from downstream. I had an eleven-foot flat bottom boat. My son and I had a good fishing trip. There are professional float trips daily through the canyon now. And of course, float fishing trips are available through the canyon. The Wind/Big Horn River is my favorite fishing river.

NO, NOT YET!

It was the middle of August and the yellow globe in the sky was sending its warm rays to me. I had been planning on this prospecting trip all week while at work. Earlier, I found a red gravel layer submerged in a dry gulch in the badlands. Taking a few gallons of classified (1/4") gravel to the lake, which was a couple miles away, I found several small flakes of gold after panning through the concentrates. I was anxious to see what amount of gold was in the gravel layer. The dry waterway that I was checking out was on BLM land. It was open to prospecting and mining. A couple weeks before, I went in and visited with BLM people and let them know where I was interested in checking out for gold. They said I was not on private land and they told me give it a shot.

I loaded up my gold pan, sniffer bottle, classifying sieve, mini high banker, sluice box, eight five-gallon buckets, two twelve-volt batteries, large hard plastic tub, and two fifty-gallon barrels of water. I was planning on staying out for eight to ten hours of hard-working fun. Taking a frozen gallon of water, a couple pops, and some snacks should take care of the hunger and thirst issues. The sky was a light blue, cloudless background indicating that it would be a very warm, dry day. Where I was going, dry was good. I drove the sixty miles to the turn off from the highway, following a weathered powerline road for a half mile to the dry gulch I wanted to work.

Reading the lay of the old creek bed, I decided the best place to get my gravel would be in front of the larger rocks where during a flash flood the gold would settle out in the slower moving water areas in front of the rocks. But first, I set up my recirculating water system to move water over by mini high banker with a sluice box extension in front of it to make sure I caught as much gold as possible. I put a little Dawn dish soap in the water. This helps break down the surface tension so the lightweight gold does not float on top of the water. I quickly classified some small gravel and fed it to the high banker which classified the material even more and let the heavier small grain material sink into the miner's moss (a sponge-like material with pores in it) which was below the ripple bars. After I run one or two five-gallon buckets of classified gravel over the high banker and sluice box, I will remove the collecting filters and rinse them out into a bucket of water. Thus, I only take home the fine collected sand to pan later.

I decided to start my gravel classifying about sixty yards in front of my set up. Then I could work my way back as the day went along. This would mean as I got tired, the shorter distance I would have to carry water to classify the gravel. Classifying the gravel includes having two five-gallon buckets of water, placing a classifier on top of a full bucket of water, and then shoveling gravel into the classifier. After three shovels of gravel, I need to shake the classifier to strain the smaller particles from the larger pea sized gravel. It is important to pour water over the gravel in the classifier to wash the gold flakes off the gravel particles. This is a slow arm tiring process. But it allows one to have higher gold recovery. Eventually, I will fill a bucket full of classified gravel. When I get two buckets full, I will carry them back to the water circulation system and using a small garden dirt scoop feed the dirt through the high banker-sluice combination.

After I cleaned out the filters for the second time, I took a small amount of the concentrate (filtered material) and panned it in the tub of water. There were a few small gold flakes in the pan as I washed away the last bit of black sand. I was very excited, as this is the first gold processing I have done. So back to work I went. After doing eight hours of this hard work in 100-degree plus temperatures, my body was getting quite tired. Thank heavens I was running out of water. Thus, after running twelve buckets of classified gravel, it was time for my final clean-up of my gold collecting apparatus.

I started collecting all my buckets and other equipment. Taking apart my water circulating system and cleaning out the water and sand from the tub continued to make me feel very tired indeed. After placing everything behind my truck, I was leaning against my truck. Those little black spots were dancing in front of my eyes and my legs and arms felt like wet noodles. Yes, I was plum tuckered out. As I leaned against the side of the truck, I noticed a shadow circulating around the top of the cab. Or was I seeing things. The shadow continued to move around in a circular pattern. Then I looked up, and in the sky above me was a turkey vulture soaring high above.

I looked at him for a short time and then said out loud, "No, not yet! I'm not that tired."

BUCK DONE GONE

It was deer season in north central Wyoming. It was especially exciting because opening day fell on Saturday. I was still a little sore from our football win the night before. But I was up early for a chance to get that large mule deer buck that was moving in and out of the badlands for food and water.

During the summer on warm sunny days, I spent parts of many days spying on the wildlife below an elevated land mass next to a small stream bordering the badlands and the farmland on the hill. The flood plain on either side of the side of the narrow creek consisted of tall grass, willow and cottonwood trees. Of course, there was a mixture of milkweed, thistle, and other weeds that needed the water to survive. Beavers also appreciated the water source for their pond making and daily routine of dam patching and food storage. And if you build a pond, then ducks and other waterfowl show up to take advantage of the marsh habitat.

I could lay upon the top of the hill elevated about fifty to seventy feet above the creek, ponds, and vegetated flood plain and watch the daily life evolve in Mother Nature's play land. Insects (some good some bad) were flying around and of course song birds and predator birds added to the environment. Below me in the tops of the Russian olive trees was a couple great horned owl nests. Magpies, a pretty black and white bird, also liked to use the Russian olive trees at a lower level to make their covered nests. These trees have sharp thorns and help protect the birds from intruders (including me).

Over the years, I have spent many days observing the area as all the animals went through their daily endeavors to create a successful environment to live in. On the far side of the stream was a large vertical sandstone cliff of around 100-150 feet high. The wind and rain over the years have created some open pockets in the side of the hill. In the middle of a large indentation about thirty feet down from the top of the cliff, a pair of golden eagles made a nest and raised their young. It was fun to watch the progressive growth of the owl and eagle chicks.

Over the years, I was able to see other animal such as porcupines, skunks, bobcats, deer, coyotes, and even a mountain lion visit the area below the hill. But at this time of the year, it is the mule deer that interested me as they come in out of the dry low food producing ground of sagebrush, greasewood, cactus, yucca, and salt grass to find water and better grazing near the creek.

Not seeing large deer in the morning, I decided to come back to the hill towards evening to watch the trails from the badland gullies. I'm sure there will be some deer come down to the creek area for food and drink. I had about an hour or so before the sun would put itself to bed, so I laid a heavy blanket down on the top of the hill and positioned myself to view the happenings of nature as it took place. The temperature started to drop as the sun descended towards the western horizon. I concentrated on a game trail that came down to the edge of the creek from a mile or so from the hills of the badlands. It wasn't long before a saw movement in the opening of the ravine straight across from my perch on the hill. It appeared to be several mule deer headed in my direction.

I slid back a little further from the edge of the hill and laid still. I could use my rifle scope to spot the deer as they followed the pathway and came closer at a slow pace. The sun being behind me allowed me to use the scope without reflection glare off the glass being spotted by the deer. It was getting cooler, but I was determined to continue my watch as the deer came closer to the flood plain area of the creek. Now, I was able to see that there was three bucks meandering down the trail. They sure were not in any hurry to get in shooting distance.

I watched and watched as they came closer to me. They were still a half mile away when I could make out that the deer in the middle was considerably larger than either deer on its side. My pulse increased as my excitement from seeing the large buck headed my way. It seemed like it was taking them forever to reach shooting range. Meanwhile, the light of day was giving way to dusk of the evening. My concern was for the buck to reach me before it became so dark that I was not able to shoot.

Slowly, the deer came closer. The large buck had a tremendous rack. It spread out on the sides of its shoulders and pointed up to the sky as if it was a shrine to Mother Nature. My excitement grew as the suspense of waiting and glassing the buck and his companions as they moved within shooting distance. I knew where they were heading and their movement would bring them within a hundred yards of my resting spot up on the hill. Another fifteen or so minutes, the huge buck deer would be mine. The nerves of my body and mind were focused in to the movement of the deer. Closer and closer they came to the creek. I was going to wait until they were very close. I did not want to miss this buck. It was the biggest one I have seen in all my days of hunting. He had been hiding out in the badlands for many years. But he was going to hide in my mom's freezer now. To show the antlers to my friends and family would be fun and just the thought of it put a large smile on my face. The time was near. I looked through the scope. Only a few more yards until the buck was near the creek and I was going to shoot. I couldn't wait much longer as daylight was fading. I wanted enough light left to dress out the deer and get it to road and loaded into my truck. I might even have to go home and get help to lift the animal into the bed of the truck. But I could probably quarter it and then get it loaded by my myself. However, I would like to get some pictures of it to show the true size of this buck.

Closer now it came. Wow! What a sight. The deer was now in sight. It was so much bigger than the other deer. I'm sure it had a lot of offspring living in the badlands and surrounding area. It was time. I adjusted my prone position and located the buck through my scope and was ready to take aim. *Oh my!* I thought. *What was that loud noise?* The buck raised its head at the same time as I turned to see a green pickup with no muffler heading straight for me. I quickly looked back at the deer and they were headed back to the badlands at a very fast pace.

The pickup door slams and my good buddy comes walking up to me and says, "Have you see any deer this evening?"

BALD EAGLES LIKE FISH

I was fishing in my boat on Upper Sunshine Lake. This a wonderful fishery. It is a favorite spot for camping and fishing for residents from Meeteetse, Wyoming or for us adopted fisherman across the Big Horn Basin region. The is an elevated lake that serves as a recreation area and as a storage bin for irrigation water for the ranchers and farmers of the surrounding region. The upper lake is drained to help fill the lower lake which is drained during farming season when more water is used. Both lakes are left full enough to be a good fishery all year around.

One warm afternoon, my granddaughter and I were trolling for some Yellowstone cutthroat trout. This a very tasty trout with nice pink/red meat. People really enjoy the fish fixed in many different recipes. On the southeast corner of the lake, a high cliff protrudes up above the water. It is known as The Proventil Bluff or Eagle Cliff by the fishermen.

As we were trolling towards the bluff, I noticed two eagles perched on top of the cliff. We were looking at them through binoculars. They seemed to be resting and enjoying the warmth of the day. We have seen the eagles around the lake many times over the years. As we approached closer to the cliff, they both lifted off in flight. They flew towards us and then swooped down to the water and both eagles hit the top of the water with their talons and up over our heads they flew with a fish clutched in those talons. It was quite a sight to see. I only wish I would have had a movie camera to record the eagles in action.

A few years later, I was ice fishing on the lake. The ice was clear of most of the snow. The temperature was around twenty-five degrees and very little wind was present. A very nice day for ice fishing. I noticed some fish guts frozen to the top of the ice not very far from where I had drilled my two holes through the ice. After I set up my fishing poles with bait, I set down in my chair to wait for the fish to come for their lunch. After catching a few fish and releasing them back into the water unhurt, I waited for a bigger fish to take my bait. I noticed a shadow on the ice. I looked up to see a bald eagle flying over my head heading towards the east end of the lake. I thought he was probably headed for Eagle Cliff. I went back to pole watching. I happened to be looking at the right time as the eagle came soaring down and tried to pick up the fish remains off the ice. His talons grabbed for the meat, but it was frozen too hard to the ice. After the eagle flew by, I walked over and kicked the remains as rough as I could and finally dislodged a large chunk.

I picked up the fish guts and carried them over to where I was fishing. I tossed the fish innards behind me about thirty feet. I then went back to catching the big one. After catching a couple fish, I had kind of forgotten about the guts and the eagle. I heard a click-click on the ice behind me. When I turned around, I saw the eagle pecking at the innards. The he picked them up with his talons and flew off towards the mountains to the south of the lake. It was quite the sight to see the eagle up close as he indulged in a snack. I was amazed at his gracefulness as he flew off to the mountains on the south side of the lake. Again, a camera would have been nice to have.

Another time on the lake, as I was trolling along out from the shore fishermen, I spotted a bald eagle perched on a pole that was not far from the people fishing off the bank. It sure didn't seem afraid of the human presence. I think all was fine if nobody made any sudden movements towards the eagle. I made a pass by the shore and the eagle and was on my way back when I saw the eagle swoop down and big up a hurt fish that was floating on top of the water. It is a wonderful sight to watch an eagle in the wild. It is really a nice to see it in action.

While driving over to the lake to go fishing, I saw some rabbit roadkill stretched out on the road. A group of crows were having a good time making it their lunch. As I approached in my pickup, they looked at me in scorn and flew off to the side of the road to come right back after I passed the dead rabbit.

It was getting dark as I approached the same area where earlier I saw the rabbit laying on the road. Sure enough, a big dark blob appeared in front of me on the road. Well, I speeded up a little to scare the crows. To my surprise, A big golden eagle flew up in front of me. I'm the one who was surprised. I was afraid he was going to come through the window. He did cause an eclipse of the window as he soared up over the top of my truck. It is safe to say that I did not approach any roadkill in a thoughtless way again. Them their eagles have a wide wing span. I'm a witness to that.

WATCH WHERE YOU ARE STEPPING

When I was in middle school in Byron, Wyoming, I was an avid animal watcher. I really liked to lay on a hillside and watch the wildlife as they went about their daily routines. I got to see a variety of interesting shows put on by the local animals. There were many animals willing to let me watch them. Of course, most of the time, they were not aware of me spying on them. Any way they let me think that way. One day while I was walking through some high grass on the flood plain of Coon Creek; I observed the great horned owl nests in the tops of several Russian olive trees. I knew it was time for the young to in the nests. I was walking slowly on this nice warm summer day. As I was walking through the grass, I spotted a lid to a fifty-gallon barrel sitting on a slant in the tall grass. Being a youngster of Tom Sawyer style, I couldn't help stepping down on the lid because it was there. To my surprise, my foot continued forward on the lid. The lid was moving out from under my foot. Of course, my blood ran cold. A lid was not supposed to go a walking with you. Then I saw a porcupine crawl out from under the lid. He acted as if he was still half asleep from his nap. He didn't even look back at me. He just meandered down the trail in front of me. About sloth speed, I think.

Another time, I was stepping over the side of the hill along the flood plain of the Wind River south of Thermopolis, Wyoming. I wanted to get down to the river to reach one of my favorite fishing holes. As I stepped over the top of some sagebrush, my foot rolled as something rolled off from under my foot. A couple very large bull snakes were laying on the side of the hill sun bathing.

My heart skipped a beat as my first thought was rattlesnakes. But a close look allowed me to look closer to the yellower color and rattle less features of the bull snake. Again, they did not seem to want to slither away. They just wanted me to get out of their sunlight. So, I did just that. I mentioned that it was nice to see them and wished them a good day. I ventured off to the river below to catch some nice trout.

LIGHTS-CAMERA-ACTION

I was fishing one of my favorite fishing spots. This was an upper camp ground region upstream from the Wind River Canyon south of Thermopolis, Wyoming. The low water river affords several nice spots to catch fish. There are fast moving rapids and slow regions caused by back-whirls on the stream's corners.

It seems like there is always something going on during the summer around this stretch of the river. The two picnic areas are used by individuals camping or maybe just stopping to eat a quick lunch as they are traveling to the Teton or Yellowstone Parks. A local guided rafting company produces fishing float trips and whitewater rafting trips through this part of the river and downstream through the beautiful Wind River Canyon.

When traffic is high in this area with fisherman, I take to the steep cliffs along the side of the river to move down the far side of the river from the other people crowding the banks. On the far side where the steep bank is located there are no kids, dogs, or vehicle traffic. One can drive a four-wheel drive old road to get to the spot I like to fish. After walking down a game trail on the steep bank, I can either fish a small back-whirl area which is usually worth at least one nice rainbow or brown trout or maybe even both.

The water level was a little too high for me to wade along the edge of the river, so I decided to play mountain goat and walk along talus of the steep edge of the high bank about twenty-feet up from the water and about ten feet from the top of the bank. There was no trail to follow. Therefore, the walking was slow. I had to be very careful with my footing. Stepping on the side of my feet, I was able to work my way along the edge stopping often to get my balance and cast out in the faster moving water and reeling back in through the slower water along the shoreline. I managed to catch three nice fish. I put them on a stringer. I clipped the stinger to my belt.

I stopped at one spot that allowed me to grab a hold of some weeds to support myself as I casted. This was a precarious position to say the least. I heard talking and laughing come from up stream. I looked up the river to see three large rafts full of six to eight people. They were decorated out in their clean clothes unlike my muddy, fish-smelling pants. They all had on a nice orange or blue life jacket. I was standing up high on the hillside with my fish stringer hooked to my belt with those three fish attached. My fishing pole was in one hand as I was holding on to some weeds to balance myself with the other hand. I was trying to set the hook on another fish.

Little did I know that it was almost show time. As the rafts came down the river right above me, the weeds came loose, and I was sliding down the bank into the waiting river below. The tourist on the rafts were using their cameras with genuine excitement and enthusiasm as I fell into the water. I sprang up and stood there showing my fish in one hand and raising my pole with the other. The rafts floated on by. But I'm sure I made some of the tourist's vacation movies or "Look what we saw" pictures of their trip. There was a lot of laughter and giggling going on as the raft people pointed and waved as they moved on down the river. I smiled and signaled my showmanship as well. It was certainly a lasting memory for me.

THUMP ON THE ROOF

On a nice warm summer day, I was helping my dad load the burn barrels in to the back of our pickup. It was time to empty the contents in our dumping area in a small ravine close to the badlands. Before I left, my mom asked me to stop along the ditch bank and pick some fresh asparagus for supper. To get to the dump, I had to travel on an old dirt road which ran along the edge of our alfalfa and sugar beet fields.

In the past, someone must have raised asparagus for the cannery which was about twenty miles away. The canary was on its dying days. It still took corn and beans but was about to close because of its old age and farmers were turning to other crops. In my younger years, my brother and I would go out and pick ten to fifteen gallons of asparagus off our ditch banks, clean and package it. Then we would take it in to our small town and sell it door to door. It was a good way to make a little money. Our mom was good at helping us in our business adventures.

I was sure willing to pick some asparagus. It was one of my favorite vegetables to eat. So, I jumped into the pickup and headed up the old dirt road. Since it was quite warm, I decided to pull up under a large cottonwood tree along the fence line. This allowed the pickup and barrels some shade and stopped them from getting hot while I was busy picking the asparagus. I pulled up under the long branches of the large cottonwood tree. As I stopped the truck and turned off the engine, a loud thump sounded on the roof of the truck. I was not sure what happened to make the sound. It really didn't sound like a limb falling on the metallic roof. The sound was too soft and yet you could tell the falling object had some weight.

Without waiting very long, I slowly opened the door and looked up at the roof of the pickup. Then, I saw the object of the sound. A large bobcat was staring right at me. It was no further than a couple feet away. We looked at each other for a few quick seconds and then we both realized that we were scared. I jump back! The bobcat jumped down on the hood of the pickup and bounded away through the alfalfa field across the road. I watched as it ran out of sight. He was beauty in motion as his graceful muscles moved him to safety. I picked the asparagus and emptied the trash barrels and then headed home to tell anyone who would listen about my little adventurous trip. To this day, I can still see the look on the bobcat's face as he seemed to be laughing at my reaction. Chalk up one "gotcha" for the cat.

OH, HELLOW THERE!

In my high school days, I had a couple "hello there" days as I was enjoying Mother Nature. These days occurred back in the mid-sixties before the reintroduction of the wolves into Yellowstone Park. Throughout my experiences with nature through the sixties, I had the pleasure of seeing a couple animals that were very rare to witness at that time in our river bottom land or anywhere within a hundred miles. I lived about 100-miles from the south entrance to Yellowstone Park.

One of my favorite places to frequent during the summer or winter was the three beaver ponds below a hill where our irrigation water ran off the hill and formed the ponds between the hill and the Shoshoni River that was only a hundred yards from the hill. This produced a tremendous area to observe wildlife, look for glaciated rocks left behind or even make forts and do a lot of pretending. It was the ideal place to be raised.

It was close to Christmas time. I was a junior in high school when I was down on one of the frozen ponds. I pick up a stick as my hockey stick and used other small twigs as my pucks and was hitting the pucks towards a stick outlined goal a little further down the pond. The ice was clear and the pucks slid down the ice easily.

After my hockey game was over, I started to go towards the river to see what might appear in that direction. I had to follow a game trail through the high cattail and willow plants surrounding the pond. I had only gone twenty or thirty yards down the trail and turn towards the river when a lynx appeared right in the middle of the path, no more than twenty feet away. Now I know the difference between a bobcat and a lynx. The cat was light colored with the identifying black hair above its ears. It was also bigger than the bobcats that I had seen over the years. The lynx looked at me as if he wanted to play the Little John and Robin Hood routine for the right of passage on the trail. We just stared at each as to say hello and then we parted company each going different directions. This was probably a once in lifetime sighting. What a beautiful animal in its winter coat.

It was deer hunting season in the mid-sixties on the river bottom. I was a senior in high school. The area I liked to hunt deer was a tree covered section of land that was located between the Shoshoni River and some irrigated open fields. The deer were well protected and out of sight in the wooded region. I was moving through the trees when I saw a nice mule deer buck move ahead of me. He was following the game trail that ran up stream along the river. I put it in sneak and stalked very slowly and quietly as I narrowed the distance between us.

As I got closer to the deer, he either saw me or smelled me. He started moving faster through the trees. Having hunted this area over the years, I knew where he was headed. I moved in a cut-off direction to intersect the deer. This forested area had met lighting or farmers burning their fields many times over the years. There was not much under-growth among the trees. This allowed me to run up another trail. As I was using my track star speed to round some willows, I came to a screeching halt. Right before my very eyes was a wolf standing over his venison lunch. I thought it was only in the movies that the wolf stood snarling as he showed his pretty whites. This growling snarl registered quickly upon my scared body. I was in a quick hurry to say hello and venture in a different direction.

On Monday morning in school, I informed my friends of seeing a wolf down on the river bottom. They snarled and laughed at me. Nobody believed there were wolves anywhere close to our little town. I kept telling them what I saw. I have seen many coyotes over the years. Believe me I know the difference between a coyote and a wolf, especially their teeth. A week later, my buddy came to me in the hallway and told me he saw a wolf in the same area as he was hunting over the weekend. To my knowledge, that was the only sighting of a wolf on our river bottom. I will never forget the look of those jaws and teeth letting me know that I was not welcome to share his lunch.

A FISHING WE WILL GO

It was a warm late summer day in 1988 when my family decided to make a one-day fishing trip to Lily Lake. The lake had a rather rare fish species for Wyoming. The grayling was a fish I had not caught before. It was time to do so.

Loading up my 1978 two-wheel drive pickup with fishing and picnic materials, my wife Linda, and three kids (Jon-fifteen, Cameron-nine, Marie-eight), we headed up to the Big Horn mountains. I knew of a back road into the lake (short cut-smile-smile). The road ran along the top of a hillside overlooking the Lily Lake watershed. A nice-looking grass meadow dotted with a generous amount of granite boulders covered the western face of the hillside. It was a sight that would make a good-looking jigsaw puzzle.

We could see the lake three-quarters of a mile below. A fence line had been built between the four-wheeled drive road going down to the lake and the lake itself. Not wanting to drive back to the main road and take the long way around, I decided we would drive until we were parallel to the lake and then walk the 300 yards over to the lake. My pickup has a low-speed rear end and can climb quite well. I had taken it hunting many times. Well, down the hill we went.

As we got closer to the lake, I could see that there was a lot more boulders that were hiding under the tall grass. But I wanted a grayling so we continued to move towards the lake. Then it was time to stop and think things over. Maybe this route was not such a good idea after all. We stopped and had our picnic, which was good. Now what to our eyes did we see, but rain clouds forming in the afternoon sky. The decision was made to start back out before the rain came. If the hillside got wet, the truck would have less traction on the hillside going out.

I turned the truck around and we started up the side of the hill. It was slow going. I had my son walk in front of the truck to guide me over and around the boulders. Then my truck ended up high centered on a granite rock. Not good! Then the misty rain came. Strike two. We all tried to push and shove the truck off the rock. The grass was getting damp and I knew we were in a sticky situation. Cameron has asthma and only brought an inhaler which was low. The girls were trying to be positive, but panic wasn't far away. Linda and I both needed to be at work the next day. While rocking the truck back and forth shifting from low to reverse, the floor shifting lever came off in my hand. Strike three.

Now frustration and panic were settling in everyone. Cameron was having a light asthma attack. Marie was having a slight crying attack. My wife was having a slight angry-at-me attack. Jon was having a "What are we going to do?" attack. I was having "a hundred things going through my mind" attack. It was for sure that we were going to spend the night on the mountain. It was a good thing we always had sleeping bags in the back of the truck. The truck had a camper shell on it, so we were able to stay warm. We still had some cookies and hot dogs and chips left from the picnic to munch on. We also had a gallon of water to drink.

The morning brought sunny, dry weather. I pulled the covering off the shifting lever on the floor. Found a pin sitting on the floor. The pin had come out disconnecting the lever. I was able to put the shifting assembly back together. Jon and I took a hatchet and hammer and chipped some of the rock off. With Cameron driving and the rest of us pushing on the front of the truck. Luck was with us as we were able to back off the boulder. Then we loaded everything up in the truck and started up the mountain side. Jon did a good job of guiding me between the boulders and the good mold green pickup climbed up to the top and we were back on the road heading to town.

The trip created some serious moments. After getting back on the road, smiles and laughter became more numerous. Many laughs from telling the story for years afterward provided memories for all of us.

GREENHORN HUNTERS

My first attempt at applying for a moose permit was a success. I was excited to draw the hunting permit. A lot of my friends have been applying for years and have not drawn a permit. The season was in the middle of September. The weather in Wyoming is often still warm and snowless. This year has been quite mild so far.

I borrowed a tent and a couple cots from my National Guard company. It helped that I was supply sergeant. I had a well-used 1978 Ford two-wheeled drive pickup. The pickup had a low-speed rear end and a rebuilt engine. Thus, it could climb and did run quite well.

I talked my brother Gene into going with me. The season opened on a Saturday. This was good as I had a football game on Friday afternoon. We could leave on Friday evening and travel the two hundred miles to Turpin Meadows. Turpin Meadows was located at the top of the Wind River mountain range in northwestern Wyoming. It was not far from the Teton National Park. The elevation was around ten-thousand feet.

The weather has been in the low to mid-sixties all week. Gene and I packed light camping gear. The supplies included: sleeping bags, tent, cots, flashlights, light coats, lantern, Coleman stove, gloves, and, of course, food and drink. We were looking for a nice couple of days hunting in the mountains. I had to get back on Monday for school. We were leaving at our elevation of 4,400 feet to drive up to Togwatee pass at about 10,000 feet. I've driven over this pass a couple times over the years. I stopped off at the local national forest office and obtained a map of the Turpin area. I wanted to know where the right turn-off was located and where the side roads in the area was located.

Friday afternoon, we won our football game and I let my assistant coach handle the post-game duties. After talking to my players and a couple parents, I was on my way home. The small town (Ten Sleep) I coached and taught in was twenty-six miles from Worland. I wanted to get going towards the mountains as soon as possible, I knew Gene would have the pickup loaded when I got home. It was nice to have a camper shell on the pickup. This would help keep everything dry if we did see some rain.

Gene and I were looking forward to a nice couple of days in the mountains. As we were driving down the road, we saw a few antelope and a couple mule deer. Once we left Riverton, we headed out of the temperate desert and started towards the beautiful town of Dubois which was located at the base of the Wind River mountains. Dubois is an old western town with all the tourist fixings. We stopped for a quick supper and then got back on the road. We didn't notice how the sky was becoming more blanketed by clouds.

As we climbed up the mountains, we saw an increase in the cloud cover and a decrease in the sunshine as it was getting late afternoon. Being a science teacher, I knew the temperature usually dropped five degrees for every thousand feet in elevation you climbed. But who was thinking about that now when you could tell stories and think of the moose you wanted to harvest?

As we continued to ascend the mountain, the sky turned gray and it started to sprinkle. We continued to drive up the mountain as the temperature outside seemed to decrease. To our surprise as we came within a few miles of the Turpin Meadows turn-off, it started to drop a light snow. By the time we turned off and started down to the meadow region, the snow was no longer light. It was coming down in big pillow feather sized flakes. We drove up one road a short distance and we found a sign telling us that it was a private road and no camping was allowed. Luckily, there was enough room to turn around. Back down to the main road we went. By now, the ground and road were covered with the white fluff from the sky. It was coming down so hard it was hard to see where you were going.

We started up another road. There were other campers there and it was a dead end. So back down the road we went. About a half-mile down the main road, we found a flat area off to the side of the road. This was going to be our home. We opened the back of the pickup and took out the tent and using my skill that I obtained over the years in the National Guard and Gene's Air Force experience, we got the tent put up. Unloading the cots and sleeping bags into the tent was next. The lantern gave us some light in the tent. Meanwhile, Mother Nature was dumping snow from the heavens in large amounts. In time, it was still early in the night. What is one to do? We did not bring any heat except our Coleman stove. We knew it was not healthy to burn the stove in the tent. The build-up of gases would not be healthy. We had a sandwich and some pop and then tried to plan our hunt for the next day.

Eventually, we crawled into our sleeping bags and tried to sleep the night away. It was earlier than normal for us to sleep, but what is one to do when the snow is falling as if a dump truck is dropping its load. It was a cold dark night inside of the tent. When we woke up in the morning and looked outside, we had to rub our eyes because we did not believe the winter wonderland sight. It was still snowing and we already had eight inches of snow. The scene was quite pretty if it would have been on a Christmas card. Not so nice if you have a two-wheel drive pickup.

We were anxious to get started looking for a moose. I had an antlerless permit. As we were getting ready to leave camp, several chained up nice new trucks passed our humble abode. They looked at us with smiles and probably a lot of laughing. We got on the main road that went around the Turpin Meadow area. We had to follow the trails where trucks had already gone. It still was not easy getting around. I did have a set of chains behind the seat. So eventually, we went back to camp. On the road that led right up behind our camp, some hunters were loading up a large cow moose into the back of Their new pickup equipped with a winch. We were both thinking. It must be nice.

After getting to our camp, we found the chains and found out they were too small for my tires. I only had the one set for the back wheels. Then I re-membered I had a roll of aluminum heavy duty wire in the back of the truck. My brother was a pretty good mechanic. I was not. After some frozen fingers and a few choice words, we were able to rig up the chains to fit the hind tires and off we were again looking for a moose. With all the snow, we were still limited to what roads we spent all day we could travel on. By mid-afternoon, there was close to a foot of snow on the roads and surrounding area. Mother Nature finally decided she had played enough of a trick on us and it quit snowing. That was good. However, if the sky cleared, it would get quite chilly during the night.

When darkness settled in, we went back to camp. We pulled out the stove and heated up some chili and made some hot dogs. We also heated up some water for hot chocolate. The hot food was good. It not only filled our stomachs, but it also warmed us up. The sky did clear and stars appeared. It did cool off quite a bit. It was dark now at five o'clock. That means we have a cold tent to wait out the night. We talked of old times and told each other stories of old adventures. Not thinking of what if, we did not bring any dry wood with us to make a fire. We sat in the truck for a couple hours keeping ourselves warm. After warming up for a while, it was time to go to our ice cave (tent). We made it through the night without getting any ice stalagmite icicles hanging from the ceiling or off our cots.

It was Sunday and we only had today to harvest our moose. After some hot chocolate and sandwiches for breakfast, we started looking around for a moose. We drove several roads as were other vehicles. We were on the main road heading back towards the highway when up in the trees on top of a hill I saw a yearling moose. I stopped the truck and got out and headed off the side of the road towards some trees. The moose continued to look at the truck. I leaned up against a tree and fired. The moose went down and I was excited. My brother finally got out of the pickup and hustled over to where I was standing. He was wondering what I saw and why I didn't give him time to see the moose also. I explained that I was not waiting around for the young moose to run away. He didn't believe that I had hit the moose.

I walked up the hillside through the snow and brush. I could not see the moose. I looked around and found its tracks. I followed the tracks, found blood, and then located the antlerless male moose calf laying in some tall brush. I was doing my moose down dance and yelling down the hill to my brother that I found the young moose. He was excited and wanted to see it. But his health was not the best. I told him to wait down by the side of the road and I would pull the moose down the side of the hill to the pickup. I pulled out my tag and filled it out. Then started to pull the moose out of the brush and begin sliding it down the side of the hill. By the time I got the moose half way down the hill, a game warden had pulled in behind my truck. He met me at the bottom of the hill. He told me that I had a nice piece of meat. I agreed.

I wish it would have been a large cow. But then, how would us two pilgrims have loaded a large animal? It would have been bigger bragging rights to come back with a large cow. But I was excited to get my first moose tag filled.

Gene and I dressed out the young bull moose. The game warden took out a tooth. He would send it to the lab to test for age and health. He also pulled the two ivory front teeth and gave them to me for a keepsake. Between the game warden, Gene, and I, we got the moose loaded onto the tarp in the back of my truck. Then we shook hands with the warden and headed back to our camp.

Once getting back to camp, we filled the open cavity of the moose with snow to help keep it cool on our way home. We decided to celebrate our success by having a good meal before we left. Gene fixed eggs, potatoes (already cooked), onions, and cut up wieners all mixed together with a side order of pork and beans. As he was cooking, I was tearing down the tent and loading up our tent and cots into the pickup. After the gourmet meal, it was time to head home. We stopped off in Thermopolis to take the moose to the meat processor. He told us that he would call me when it was ready.

I only wish we would have taken a camera. It would have helped to explain to people about our mostly fun moose expedition. Over the years, we have had quite a few chuckles over how inexperienced we were to spend a couple days in the type of weather we had on the trip. And also, about the transportation we had as we moved around on the heavy snowed roads compared to the other equipment the other hunter had. I'm sure we were the topic of conversations, as other hunters swapped stories around their nice warm comfy campfires or inside their warm campers. But as the game warden had told us, he had only seen two moose taken in the two days we were there. The moose steaks were tender and sweet and the gravy was excellent. The memories created were ones that would last a lifetime. I'm smiling and enjoying my first moose hunting adventure as I pictured our efforts to obtain my first moose.

A FISHY BEAR

Back in the day when I was in good shape and looking for adventure, I decided to hike down into Devil's Canyon. Leaving Lovell, Wyoming, it was a challenging drive up to the top of the Big Horn Mountains on a definite back country road to a spot where a person can walk down the game trail to Porcupine Creek far below. It takes twenty to thirty minutes to walk down and forty-five minutes to walk back out. From the semi-arid temperate desert at the trailhead, you can look down into the beautiful canyon below with its variety of flora and clear running water. Cottonwood trees, willows, grass, and shrubs lined the banks of the flood plain. A very nice garden which Mother Nature put together for people to enjoy.

Once I had reached the trailhead, I put my pack together and started down the game trail to the snake-like stream below. What a wonderful day for the trip. The clear blue, cloudless sky and the warm rays of the sun promised to help make the day. I was anxious to wet my line. The trip down went well. A few places were narrow. At some places a few pebbles rushed down the mountain side in front of me. Later I heard a friend of mine and his son went down this trail and my friend slipped and fell down several yards and hurt his back. His son hiked back out and got help. They flew him out and he was bruised and cut up a little and eventually healed from his ordeal. One must be careful with footing and balance.

At the bottom of the trail, I found a flat well used area to set up camp. I sat down and rested awhile. Then it was time to get my fishing pole ready to catch some fish. I was going to catch and release the fish. I placed a Panther Martin spinner on my line and set out to try my luck. Most of the vegetation along the banks of the creek were short or just grass matted the shoreline. Some places were covered by three to five-foot-high willows. The water moved along at a good shallow flow with a few deeper regions that had been carved out by flood water during high run-off times over the years. The creek was about ten to fifteen feet wide on the average.

Casting slightly up stream and letting the lure move across the creek towards me as I reeled the spinner in, it was quite effective as fish after fish attacked my offering. Wow! What a day of enjoyable fishing. The beauty of the environment and the warmth of the day provided a setting that brought smiles to my mind and face. A perfect day for enjoyment for sure! I continued to work my way down stream. Most of the fish were between eight and fourteen inches long. A combination of rainbow, cutthroat and German brown trout were hungry and found their way to my spinners as I changed my spinners to different colors and brand. They all seemed to work quite well.

I remembered that my mother-in-law would like to have some fresh fish. I never brought a creel with me. I decided to use the forked stick into the bank trick of keeping the fish alive and fresh until I was ready to leave this paradise canyon. I caught two nice size fish and stuck the forked willow through their mouths. The forked end stopped the fish from sliding off the willow. Then sticking the willow into the bank, I continued fishing. I ended up having three sticks in the bank. Each of the willows had two fish dangling from them.

As the afternoon moved on and the sun started to disappear over the rim of the canyon, I decided I had better start back towards camp. Summer days around the mountains usually brought on thunderhead clouds with rain showers. I wanted to be up the game trail and headed down the mountain before the ground became wet. The soil turns into a stick surface and footing for me and my pickup would become more challenging. I started walking back upstream to pick up my fish and pack up my gear. When I approached the first place where I had left the fish, they were gone. Thinking that they were healthy and determined to stay in the creek; I figured they wiggled their way out from the bank and went merrily on their way. I congratulated them for their efforts and headed to the next spot. When I got to the next spot, the fish were gone. Now what are the chances that both sets of fish were able to work themselves out of the bank and disappear? My mind was confused and an assortment of if's, why's and what's were running through my mind. I reached the third place where the fish SHOULD have been. You guessed it. They were gone also. Being quite surprised by the disappearance of the fish brought wonderment to my intelligence. I had my suspicions. As I rounded a small clump of willows, I spotted on the path, (almost stepping in it) a very fresh mound of bear scat. Smiling and shaking my head, I knew what had happened to my fish. Now, I start to look around for my visitor. It took no time at all. The BIG black bear was less than thirty yards from me. The bear was standing still looking back at me, I swear he had the most impish smile on his face as he thanked me for the fish. I stood still and just observed the bear. He was just standing still and waving his head around as if mocking me for my loss and his gain. I was amazed at his friendliness, but then again; he had a full stomach. I will never forget the look on his face and how that smirk told me he was not going to harm me. I was very at ease. Then after a couple minutes, the bear walked off into the taller willows along the base of the mountain.

I waited a short time and then moved past where the bear entered the willows and headed for the camp site. I did not stick around to catch more fish. I didn't want to find out if the large black bear had any hungry friends hanging around. That facial smirk and the gleam in his eyes will never leave me. It was not from fright, but one of understanding and respect. I would say the bear and I were one with each other at that moment of recognition. It was one of the most serene times I have had in Mother Nature land.

WHERE DID THEY GO?

A few years later, I returned to Devil's Canyon. The fishing and environment was just too good to pass up. This time I was planning on a two-day camping trip, I'm so impressed with the area as its beauty and variety of fish create an excellent fishing adventure. The trip up to the trailhead was awesome as the terrain was colorful and I saw many mule deer and even some sage grouse. The road was rough in some places as flash flooding from rain storms and melting snow runoff does its erosional work on the rock and soil.

The descent down the game trail went smooth. I was glad to reach the bottom and set up my camp. After eating some crackers and cheese, I got my fishing pole ready to create the fun I knew awaited. Another cloudless, warmer summer day presented perfect weather for my fishing day. With pole in hand, I advanced upon Porcupine Creek that awaited my return.

The fishing was great as I moved down stream working the holes that I was sure had fish hiding under the bank or sitting at the bottom of a deepened pocket of water which was carved out by swifter water during flood stages. I enjoyed my day of catch and release. I did keep an eye out for bears or maybe some other wildlife that may not my presence in their domain. As it was, I felt like I was the only human that knew this magnificent pristine region of the earth existed. Wow! What a day. It was starting to get toward evening. I wanted to get back towards camp and get everything ready for the evening. Set up a lean-to with a tarp and prepare some supper of soup and sandwiches.

Just before camp, I kept three fish to have for breakfast with my fried eggs. When I got back to camp, I made a rock corral in a slow-moving part of the creek to place my fish in for the night. I want to keep them fresh to tickle my taste buds. After placing the fish into the corral, I sat down and just enjoyed being part of the delightful environment that surrounded me. I've always loved the sound of a moving stream ever since my days and nights as a young boy having his Danial Boone days on the creek bottom blow our house. The sounds of nature can be so calming to my mind and body. I can't think of a better relaxing treatment. After eating and relaxing, it was time for sleep-thirty. The rains stayed away, and the night treated me well.

In the morning, I went to get the fish out of my corral. They were gone. Memories came back as when I had fish disappear on me before. I looked for animal tracks. I did not find any. I checked for any indication that the water level came up over the night. I couldn't see any proof of such. Well, an egg sandwich and some hot chocolate will serve as breakfast. I looked the area over again looking for uninvited guests to my camping area. Again, no proof of invaders was found.

I went fishing and had another wonderful day catching and releasing numerous fish that were between eight to sixteen inches in length. The German brown trout were the bigger size. They all fought well and created excellent action to see and feel. What better way to spend a day of your life? I can't think of one. The afternoon arrived with clouds forming over head in the sky. It was my signal to start making tracks for camp and leaving the canyon before the rain arrives.

I went back to camp. After loading everything in and on my backpack, it was time to hike up the steep trail out of the canyon. I stopped and looked over the rock corral, wondering what might have happened to my fish the night before. I was still puzzled by their disappearance. I looked up at the winding thin trail I had to maneuver up and my legs were not sure they wanted to make the walk, but I promised them that rest would await at the summit. As I looked up, there was several tall cottonwood trees to the left of the trail. At the top of the trees were four great-horned owls. With a smile on my face, I knew what happened to my fish the night before. I was not the only one in that wonderful canyon who liked fish.

Devil's Canyon has provided fond memories of fishing and exciting adventure. I only wish I could return to the deep canyon again. My mind says, "Yes". My legs, arms, and backs laugh and say, "No way." The body wins. But thanks for the memories.

A DOUBLE STALKING

I was a junior in high school. Deer hunting season was to open the next day. Not far from where we lived at the base of the sandhills, an old apple orchard was still fighting for existence. The apple orchard was a local hangout for mule deer. The trees, willows, and high grass were good cover. A water source was nearby. The grass and willow leaves were an adequate food source an apple for dessert wasn't bad either. The grass also made a good bedding surface for the deer.

Saturday morning, I was ready to start my walk to the orchard. Everything was a go. My rifle was an early hand me down twenty-five to thirty-five which had been deer hunting many times over three generations. It was still dark-thirty after I ate my Cheerios. After placing my hunting knife on my belt, I grabbed my coat, gloves, flashlight, and rife and was ready for the orchard. I told my mom where I was going and said that I would be back for supper. I hoped it would be sooner if I was lucky to get my deer sooner.

Just a sliver of a moon was shining. I knew my way. I've been rabbit hunting in that area a lot over the years. I've also deer hunted this region before. The walk up the old dirt road was a little scary because of past experiences with animals frequenting this semi-arid temperate desert environment. At least it was cold enough to have the rattlesnakes hibernating in their dens. I have had many adventures with the snakes. At the end of the road, I had to get across a canal that still had some water and snow in the bottom. I knew of a fence that went across the canal. The fence had a long log attached at its bottom. I was able to carefully make my way across by easing my feet along the top of the log.

Now I had to get through the barbwire fence and then start walking towards the orchard which was past a couple of bread-loaf shaped exfoliated sand hills. Past the last sandhill, it was around 300 yards to the orchard. This was open area covered with sagebrush, cactus, and yucca plants. It was still dark when I reached the last sandhill. I waited awhile until the eastern sky started to show a light gray. Then it was time to put it in sneak and move toward the orchard.

Once I was within a hundred yards of the orchard, it was light enough to observe the willow area that borders the orchard. I moved forward at a very slow pace. Staying low and being careful not to stick my hands-on cactus, I continued to move towards the apple orchard. By now my adrenaline was kicking in. I stopped for a little pause and surveyed the scene in front of me. It was very quiet and I did not see anything or anyone ahead of me. I was worried about other hunters getting there before me.

There he is! A nice big bodied four-point (some people call them eight-point) mule deer buck was moving into the willows. There are several game trails leading into the orchard. This buck had a nice sized rack. I was getting excited. With only about forty yards to the willows, I had now to crawl slowly to the willows where I saw the buck enter. I knew he had moved towards the middle of the orchard.

My senses were now getting acute and I was very hyper. The adrenaline was mounting. Carefully and quietly, I eased myself to the edge of the willows. I was about ten feet from the edge of the willows. Then all heck broke loose as a mountain lion jumped out of the willows directly in front of me. Wow! It landed within three to four feet from me. I fell back on my posterior and was shaking like a leaf in the wind. To say the mountain lion frightened, scared, and surprised me would be making light of the situation. The mountain lion was so graceful as it ran away to the east. I saw the deer heading up a hillside going into the badlands and I laid there shaking with no voice and wondering, *Did I just have that happen to me?* I believe the mountain lion and I were stalking the same deer.

After I composed myself somewhat, I decided I was going back to the house. No! I did not have to change my clothes, but I did have quite a story to tell my family.

FACE TO FACE

Our burn barrels were full. My dad asked me to put them in the back of our 1951 red pickup and empty them. I was anxious to drive the truck as I was only a freshman in high school. Dad and I loaded the two barrels. Mom also asked a favor. She wanted me to stop on the way and pick some asparagus along the ditch bank, so we could have fresh asparagus for supper. I was all for that. It was one of my favorite veggies.

After finishing my chores of feeding the chickens, milking the cow, and putting hay in the feed bunks for the horses and cows, I was ready to dump the garbage barrels. I started the truck and slowly and left the yard. The old dirt road went south along the sugar beet fields towards the badlands. About a half mile down the road, a few old cottonwood trees lined the ditch bank where some good asparagus picking awaited. Being a warm summer day, I decided I would pull under the limbs sticking out from the massive tree trunks. This would help keep the cab of the truck cooler.

When I pulled over under the low hanging limbs, I parked and turned off the truck. Then I heard a thump on top of the cab. I was startled and was worried that a branch might have fallen off the tree and dented the roof of the cab. And yet, the sound was a softer sounding noise than the solid noise a hard limb would make. I slowly inched the door of the cab open and started to get out and look to see what made the noise. As I opened the door, I looked up at the side of the door and a bobcat was looking down at me. We just stared at each other for a moment. The bobcat was as curious as I was. After a short stare down, the bobcat jumped down on the hood of the truck and bounded away towards the badlands. I just stood there trying to figure out what I just endured. It was a unique experience as our faces couldn't have been more than two feet away from each other. What a beautiful animal.

I picked the asparagus, emptied the barrels, and then was anxious to get back and inform my parents and brother of my little adventure with the bobcat.

A couple weeks later, I was rabbit hunting in the badlands. I saw a rabbit run towards an exfoliated sand rock mound. From past experiences, I knew where he was headed. I followed his path up the side of the hill stepping on natural sandstone shelves that were produced by rain, wind and ice expansion to erode the surfaces of the hill. Hurrying up the side of the hill using the sandstone steps, I was almost to the top when the rock steps broke from under my feet. I slid down from one step to another as each step gave way from my weight and momentum. As I finally came to a stop towards the bottom of the hill, the last shelf moved away under my feet. At the same time, I heard a shrill meow from the animal under my feet. I young bobcat emerged and ran away into the badlands. After calming down my nerves, I looked under the broken rock and found a partly eaten rabbit. I was sorry to disrupt the bobcat's lunch.

That winter I was playing around on a beaver pond. I was a hockey player as I was hitting a small twig around with a stick that I found along the side of the iced over pond. These ponds were very familiar to me as I laid on the top of the hill during the summer and watched Mother Nature at work. They were one of my favorite locations to spend time in the winter or summer. Today I was just goofing off and having some fun. I decided to move up to the next pond. I found the game trail that moved through the tall grass, cattails, and brush. I had only gone about thirty feet when I rounded a corner and standing in the middle of the path was a lynx. I had never saw a lynx before. They aren't normally down this low in the forty-eight states. There was no doubt. It was a lynx. I was so excited to see it. We starred at each other and just stood still. Finally, the lynx turned around and went up the trail. I decided I would go back from where I came from. I was anxious to get the half mile back to the house and inform everyone about the lynx I saw. It made my day.

I saw a couple more bobcats over the years in the badlands. They are a pretty animal and I always enjoyed seeing them in their environment. I'm glad I was not in to hunting or trapping them.

I WANT MY POLE WE BACK

My mother-in-law really liked to fish. We decided to take Saturday as our day. We knew that some catfish or maybe even a walleye were waiting to provide some exciting fishing. My wife had just given me a new fishing pole for my birthday. I was anxious to try it out. My mother-in-law (Granny, as she liked to be called) said she knew of a good spot at Yellowtail Lake that might be worthy of a try.

On Saturday morning, we left early as we wanted to spend a full day at the lake. It was only a thirty-minute drive to the lake. After going across the crossway, we turned left on a dirt road that followed the lake shoreline for about two miles. Granny pointed to a sandstone edge that stood out towards the lake where the Big Horn River laid on the bottom. I agreed that the spot look promising. A small bay was adjacent to the place we wanted to fish from.

We unloaded our fishing gear and of course some munchies. A frozen gallon jug of water would give us ample hydrate material. I let Granny pick her spot and then I put the large night crawler on my hook and casted it as far as I could. I sat the pull down and waited for a monster to bite. Granny told me that I had better anchor the pole down as a large carp may grab the bait and pull my pole into the lake. I started looking for some flat rocks and a forked stick to anchor my pole. I had barely turned to get the materials needed and Granny told me to grab my pole, I had a bite. I was too late as the pole was diving into the water in front of me. Oh my! My wife-given new pole was gone. I think I was in plenty trouble, yes!

I went back to the truck and got another pole, baited it, and casted it out. I made sure I had anchoring material before casting. We caught a couple two-pound catfish with in about an hour. I happened to glance over at the small bay. Across the other side of the bay, a carp was swimming on the surface. It seemed to stay in one place. Maybe, just maybe, that carp was hooked on the end of my fishing line. I was going to go check it out. I reeled my line in and headed for the opposite side of the bay.

When I got to the spot where I had seen the carp, I could see that it was still hovering in the same place. I took my pole and casted over where I thought the line should be and reeled the line back in. Sure enough, I had caught my other fishing line. I pulled the line towards me. Grabbing the line, started to pull the line and carp towards the shoreline in front of me. Everything was going well until the large carp decided I was not his friend. He took off with a quick jerk and snapped the line from my hand and he was gone. I waited to see where he would surface. He didn't.

Well now, I was still in trouble. I decided to see if my pole had been pulled into the bay region. I started at the shallow end of the bay and walked back and forth across the bay feeling for my line or pole. Finally, I was up to my chest in the water. I didn't want to give up. Now, it was time to start diving and feeling the bottom of the bay for my pole. I could see Granny sitting over on her perch, laughing at my efforts. That made me even more determined to find my fishing pole. It was providing entertainment for us the fish were not biting. Granny had only caught two carp since I started my search.

I had dived down in the murky water several times before I felt a rough rocky bottom. I thought that this was my last chance to find my pole. Hopefully, it was stuck between the rocks. It was getting too deep for me to go much farther towards the main part of the lake. After a couple more dives, my hand felt the pole. I grabbed a hold of it. It didn't take much to detach it from the rocks. With pole in hand, I swam back to shallower water where I was able to stand up and walk to the shore. Yelling towards Granny, I raised the pole over my head and celebrated my success.

I wasn't in too much trouble now. Just wet and hungry for picnic food. I let the sun dry me off as I returned to fishing. I held on to my pole the rest of the day. For sure, for sure!

A SMELLY CHICKEN

I had just gotten home from a two-day legion baseball trip. We won three of the four games. I played well. It was late and of course dark out. Right away my mom asked me to gather the eggs. We needed some for breakfast in the morning. I heehawed around, but it did me no good. Mom informed me that Dad would want some eggs for breakfast and of course I would also. My mom was a very good cook and I did not want to cook my own breakfast, so off to the chicken coop I went.

Carrying the egg basket, I entered the coop heading towards the rows of nest boxes along the far side of the building. Most of all the nest were occupied by a chicken sitting on the eggs. I reached under each chicken in the top row of nests and pulled the eggs from under them. The third row was about four feet above ground level. When I got to the third nest, I slid my hand under the chicken. I was a little nervous as a couple of the previous chickens had lightly pecked at my hand.

As I placed my hand under the chicken, I was not sure things felt right. Was it really feathers that I was feeling? I continued to work my hand under the chicken. Suddenly, the chicken, which was not a chicken but a skunk, exploded out of the nest. He bounced off my chest and headed quickly out the door. I'm glad he went quickly without taking the time to spray me with his well-known perfume. I didn't drop the eggs, but it was a close call. From that time on, I always took a flashlight with me to the chicken coop. Over the years I saw a raccoon, a weasel, and a fox around the chicken coop. I did have a good story to tell when I got back to the house.

A NIGHT ON THE MOUNTAIN

Yes! I was excited as I opened the fish and game envelope. I had drawn my second moose hunting permit in as many tries over the years. My friends were quite jealous as some of them had been trying from ten to thirty years and not even drawn one tag. I was feeling very fortunate to receive another tag. Getting out into nature and enjoying the scenery and of course the excitement of the hunt created strong emotions in me. I was in the middle of a football season. I was the head coach in a small school in north central Wyoming. We played our games on Friday afternoon or evening. This allowed me all weekend to do other things unless we had a junior varsity game on Saturday morning. This week we had an afternoon game (we won).

Saturday morning seen me driving to the Arizona Lake area inside the Teton National Park. This was my permit area. I wanted to go down and become familiar with the region. I also wanted to try and locate someone who had horses or mules to pack out the bull moose if I was lucky enough to shoot one. Moose are a large animal and even quartering the animal would make it very tough to pack it out of an area where you had to cover rough or uphill terrain. I purchased a good detailed map of the Arizona Lake region. I wanted to be sure of the turn off dirt road to the trailhead going down into the lake area. The 200-mile drive south to the Teton park was a nice ride. I was familiar with most of the trip. We traveled most the route as we played football against Dubois which is found in a nice valley at the base of part of the wonderful Rocky Mountain range. I have always enjoyed the western buildings and lifestyle of the town. It is surrounded by the red iron filled hills which provide a nice contrast to the coniferous and deciduous flora. From Dubois, the route means a beautiful drive up the mountain to Togwatee Pass and down to Moran Junction. The road is a narrow highway which seems to always be under construction processes. The scenery is great. The forest with its variety of plants such as the pine trees, spruce trees, willows, grasses, and flowers create a beautiful nature bouquet. The clean crisp late summer air with the light blue cloud scattered sky adds to the enjoyable trip over the mountain. Then you drop down into the temperate desert valley with its sagebrush-grass flora.

At Moran Junction, you have the choice of either going to Jackson or to the Teton Park. I turned right and headed to the Teton park. The Teton mountains were majestic as a background for my journey. On the southern side of the road, nice clear fresh water creek meandered its way through the picturesque valley. Maybe it was a good omen as I saw a cow and calf moose eating willow leaves on the grassy flood plain. I continued towards the lake enjoying the mixture of the different types of flora and fauna of the desert-mountain environment. There were rustic cabins and some small ranches setting back on the north side of the road nestled on the flat base of the mountains. I saw a cabin and corrals sitting back away from the road. I drove down the dirt road to the house. I saw that a couple horses were in the corral. As I turned off the motor to my truck, as if on cue, a man walked from the corral area. He was dressed as if he was a century in the past. We introduced ourselves and shook hands. I informed him that I was going to come down in two weeks to go moose hunting in the Arizona Lake drainage. I was looking for someone to pack out the big bullwinkle moose after he met his fate by my hands. Bruce said he knew the area and would be glad to pack the moose out. We settled the monetary business and shook hands again. I returned to my truck and was headed to the Arizona Lake turn off. I had to go through the Teton Park entry check station. I told them where I was heading and my intentions. After paying the entry fee, I started looking for the dirt road that would lead me to the trailhead.

The rancher had told me how far from the entry port the road was and what country would look like as the turn off approached. To my surprise, I spotted the correct turnoff and head down the narrow, rough weather eroded road. After a mile or so, I pulled up to the trailhead parking area. The first thing I noticed was a sign letting me know that I was in grizzly country. That sign always causes my blood to chill. I saw what had to be the trail up the wooded hillside to Arizona Lake. I was excited to scout the area. However, I had a very sore hoof as I have had a lot of trouble with my right ankle. I've been working out hard to get myself into great shape to go to staff sergeant school for the National Guards. I had one year left to retirement. Cartilage breakdown, bone spurs, and bone chips have caused a lot of pain lately. Sometimes a bone chip lodges just right and my ankle feels like it is full of razor blades. But being tough and determined, I was going to climb up the trail and get a look at the region I was to hunt. Later, I did go to school, passed the class, and retired as an E-6. I also had my ankle operated on after I retired from the service. That operation leads to another story. I died from shock for twenty-four minutes, but all did turn out okay.

The trail up the mountain side was a drainage area for the small region. There were down trees and large rocks which caused me to skirt around and climb up the bank of the flow area. This caused my ankle to say a few choice words to me. But I continued my climb up the 500 yards to the crest of the hill. From there, I could see the meadow below with Arizona Lake and the tree line circling the lake. The west side of the lake was bordered by a thick forest. There were signs on the tree trunks that indicated that the lake side was wilderness. I can hunt only the wilderness area. The east side of the lake had a few yards of grass before you entered the forest. Looking through my field glasses, I could see a nice willow patch at the far end of the lake. I would think that would make a good spot for moose to lay down and even grab a snack. I studied the scene in front of me for a while and then started back down the trail to the trailhead.

By the time I reached the pickup, my ankle was chattering quite extensively. But it would calm down on the way home. The weather continued to be nice and the ride home was enjoyable, observing the surroundings that Mother Nature provided created contentment. It was dark thirty before I arrived home. Then it was time to make some phone calls. I want a couple friends of mine to go with me. As time for the opening day of moose hunting season approached, I had recruited my brother-in-law Gordon and my best friend Mike to go with me.

The Friday before I was leaving for the hunt, we played an afternoon football game. We won so I was a happy camper. After getting all the post-game duties taken care of, I hurried home anxious to get everything loaded into the trucks for the trip. Mike, Gordon and our wives had gathered up the goodies and all we had to do was load stuff from the house and lawn. After tarping the trucks, we said good-bye to our wives and headed down the road. Of course, I had to cover all the details of the football game. The win had put us in a good position to win the conference title (which we did). Mike rode with me and Gordon drove his own truck down. We had to make tracks, as it was going to get dark before we got to the Arizona Lake trailhead. The drive down was uneventful as we talked about the upcoming hunt and we made good time. Going through Dubois was nice as always. We stopped and got sandwiches to go and moved along. The drive up the mountain was good, except for the construction area. It was getting dark as the sky was overcast and a slight drizzle presented itself. We were happy to see Moran Junction. Off to the trailhead we go. The terrain looks different a night. I was the only one that knew where I thought I was going. Of course, we missed the turn-off the first time. But we turned around and found the correct road to lead us to the trailhead.

We parked the trucks, put the food coolers in the trucks, and had some cookies and cola. Then we wanted to get some sleep, so we would be fresh for the morning hunt. We slept in the trucks (quite crowded). But being so excited for the next day to arrive, we handled it. Brrrr, the morning was a little chilly, but again, who cares? A-hunting we will go. We did not have any grizzly visitors through the night. When the sky was just peeling back its black blanket, we were getting ready to start up the trail. My ankle was a little stiff and sore from being cramped up in the truck. As the ground was a little damp, we looked for grizzly or any other animal tracks. The only tracks we saw were from a couple deer that must have come through the parking area during the night. Both Gordon and Mike commented on the signs about possible grizzly bears in the area. From past experiences, we know that grizzly bears have learned that a rifle shot means food is on the table. In fact, a couple years earlier I was hunting with several people up in a mountain region called Sunlight Basin. This area borders Yellowstone Park. One of the guys shot a cow elk. By the time we dressed the elk out, two grizzly bears let us know that we were messing with their dinner. Well, we apologized and moved slowly away from the table and left that area.

Putting all bear-attracting material inside the trucks, we started up the trail. Weaving in and out of the blockage material (rocks and down trees), we steadily climbed up the hill. Finally, we reached a large rock with its side kick, a downed pine tree. I knew this was almost the crest of the trail. After another thirty yards, we were looking down at Arizona Lake and its beautiful water surrounded by the thick forest on the west shoreline and the grassy shoreline on the east side. We discussed our strategy. It was decided once we got to the bottom of the hill, Mike and Gordon would work their way along the west side of the lake. They might scare something out towards me as I went down the east side. So, we started down the mountain. As if on cue, a bone chip shifted in my ankle and the dance was on.

As we reached the bottom, a couple of hunters approached us. They were riding horses. We asked if they had seen any moose. They had seen a cow and calf when they first started out. But it was still dark and besides they had a bull permit. That was not good news seeing them come from the direction I was headed. I would assume they might have scared away any game along the trail. They moved on after we wished each other good luck. I had to cross a small creek and find a trail just inside of the tree border, so I could see the whole area surrounding Arizona Lake. Mike and Gordon gave me a head start before they started making noise as they worked their way through the heavily wooded area on the west side of the lake. With our orange vests, we could see each other clearly as we moved north towards the other end of the lake.

The lake was approximately 100-150 yards wide and maybe 1,200-1,500 yards long. The trail found lead along the east side of the lake. It was not a smooth country road. The tree roots, shallow grass bogs, and rocks triggered SOS pain messages through my ankle. But adrenaline was doing its part to counter attack. At one point, I came to what looked like a narrow, shallow spring creek which drained into the lake. I decided to wade across the spring. Wow! I stepped off into the water up to my chest. What a sudden surprise. I lifted the rifle up over my head and with a couple of steps, I was to the other side crawling out. Then I looked over to see Mike and Gordon doing a country jig. They were trying to get my attention. They were pointing at the group of willows straight in front of me.

There he was in all his Bullwinkle-ness. A large bull moose stood looking at my buddies. He had not noticed me. My National Guard expert marksmanship training told me to get down in a good prone position and prepare to take aim. I did. Taking a breath, exhaling and slowly squeezing the trigger; one shot. The moose some 300 yards off, turned a somersault, and disappeared off into the willows. I was so excited. I knew I had hit him. By the time I arrived on the willow scene, Gordon and Mike had just reached the area also. Mike was wet up to his waist. He had found one of those shallow spring creeks also. We looked around and did not see the moose. I was confused. I walked back to half the distant from where I shot from. Then lined up the line of sight of the rifle shot. We were looking at the wrong tuff of willows. I walked back to the willows and seen some blood on the grass. Then twenty feet away there he laid. I let out a yelp and went into my invented moose dance. What sore ankle. Adrenaline was in charge now. We were smiling big time. Shaking hands, they congratulated me several times. They told me about their run in with the shallow (deep) small creek. It was funny now, but not so funny as it was happening. I agreed with their assessment of that experience.

We dressed out the moose. Then quartered it. Mike and I thought we might try packing out a front quarter. I found a ten-foot pole and we tied the quarter on it and put the pole on our shoulders and headed out. We made all of two yards. No way! Even on a good ankle, it was not happening. Mike and Gordon were going to finish quartering and skinning the moose, so it would cool. I was going to go notify the rancher about my bull moose. We would get him in here and get out while it was still light. It was only about ten o'clock in the morning. I started out of the willows to find the south trail leading to the path going back to the trailhead. The trail through the forest was up and down with areas close to the lake (they were swampy) and other areas that lead away from the lake. They were hilly and forested. My natural pain reliever (adrenalin) was backing off and my ankle was letting me know I was not his friend. But one must do what one must do. Eventually, I got to the small creek and recognized the beaver dam I crossed earlier in the morning. After crossing the dam, I started up the hill towards my truck.

After reaching the truck, I loosened my shoe lace and took off some of the pressure on my ankle. On my way to the rancher's place, I ate some cookies and chips and drank some water. I was tired, but a happy smile was on my face. I reached the turn off into his place. Driving up the road, I did not see his truck there. I parked the truck, got out and looked around. I did not find anyone at home. I panicked. How was I going to get that large moose out of that valley? I started driving around to each place I good to see if they could help me. The answer was always the same. There were some forest fires burning on the other side of the Teton Lake and the ranchers who had horses or mules had leased them out to the forest service to help fight the fires. By now, I was in a pinch. I figured I had better get back to my friends and the moose. I knew I had to leave it down there overnight. I stopped off at the general store to get some ammonia. I had heard that placing a tarp over the game with ammonia poured on it or even placing moth balls on the tarp would help prevent bears from messing with the meat. The problem was that the store did not have either one.

I drove back to the trailhead. After talking my ankle in to going up and down the mountain again, I grabbed a tarp and my flashlight. I started towards my moose and friends. It was still warm. I never thought about putting on warmer clothes or even taking rain gear with me. I was not aware of how late it was. As I limped my way down the trail towards the moose, I could tell late afternoon was sneaking up on me. I took the trail in the forest trying to stay away from ruts and bogs. I finally made it back to the willow area. My friends were not there. I guess they wanted to get out of there before dark. They were not familiar with the trail my side of the lake. I don't know how we missed each other as we must have passed somewhere on my way down.

I placed the tarp on the moose meat. Not being able to obtain the moth balls or ammonia, decided to urinate on the tarp. Maybe human smell would keep the bears away. I started back out. Clouds appeared. It started to drizzle. Darkness hit as I was about half way back to the south end of the lake. By this time, my ankle felt like it was broken. I could hardly walk. My flashlight was not producing much light. My body was starting to feel the coolness of the rain, trying to find my way back in the dark was not working out very well. I must have moved off further into the forest. I tried to get back to the lake. I was unable to find the path back to the lake. Then I figured I had gone too far south. I ran into another pond and a very boggy area. These bogs caused me to twist my ankle and I tripped and fell down several times. I was getting wet from the misty rain. My ankle was extremely sensitive, and walking was becoming very difficult.

As I was making my way through the willows, I would be showered by the water off the tops of the willows. This made me very cold. Then the thought of hypothermia entered my mind. Quickly panic started setting in. What was

I going to do? Then I heard a lot noise in the willows close to me. I knew there was something there. I stood quietly and listened carefully. Then I heard a splash. I figured I had spooked out a moose. I hoped it was a moose. It started to sprinkle harder and I realized I was lost. I should have stayed where I was and looked for some shelter. But I continued to access my situation and thought I could find my way to the trail.

I started back north towards where I thought lake was. I continued to slip; twisting my ankle. I continued to move through willows that covered me with water. At some point, I'm sure shock set in. I was wandering along not sure where I was. Finally, I realized that the highway was west of where I was. I headed that way. I was on drier land. I was still tripping as a pulled my right leg along. I have been getting drenched as the brush kept drenching me with moisture. I looked at my watch. It was two o'clock in the morning. This means I have been wandering around for over six hours back and forth trying to find the trail leading up the mountain to the trailhead. I walked several more yards and came to a swamp of cattails and water. I decided it was time to hold up for the night. I broke off some tops of small trees and tried to make a shelter by putting branches on top of some brush. I wanted to just get out of the steady light rain. I could not walk any further. I was tired and very depressed. Panic fed by the thought of grizzlies and hypothermia was creating much worry. I got under the shelter, if that is what you want to call it. It was better than walking through willows. I hugged my incandescent type flashlight. Oh, how I wished it would furnish some heat. As I sat there on the ground with all kinds of weird thoughts going through my mind, such as family, friends, endeavors of the past; I was shaking so bad. I could not quit shivering. Since I was a biology teacher, I knew the shaking was critical to keep my body warmer. But I also know how the cold can affect a person, I knew I could not go to sleep. I talked out loud, I counted, I tried different things to keep me awake. I just knew I was not going to let myself sleep. And of course, in the back of my mind; was the thought that I was in grizzly country.

To my somewhat relief, daylight finally arrived. I was stiff and sore. Slowly I got up and stretched my arms and legs. I looked around me to try and get my bearings. I thought I knew where! was. I could see the mountain side off to my left. On the other side of the mountain was the trailhead. I turned back towards the east to get away from the swamp. I went around a group of willows and almost stepped in a pile of fresh bear scat. I froze. I had only gone a few yards from where I spent the night. Then I heard something going through the cattails off to the side of me. I could see the back end of a grizzly moving into the cattails. I started moving slowly back to where I thought I had to go. To my surprise, I was very close to the moose. I walked over to it and it was okay.

I started walking back along the east side to the lake. I knew the trail up the mountain was somewhere in that direction. I walked and walked. I limped and limped. I finally found myself at the base of the mountain. I still was not sure where I was. I happened to look down and saw a blue hair tie laying on the ground. I picked it up. I looked up at the side of the mountain. There was a slight crease in the hill side. I told myself that the highway was somewhere in that direction. I was going to climb the mountain at this point no matter what.

I climbed very slowly as I was tired, sore and unsure where I was going. Eventually I saw a tree with a large rock friend. Then I heard a well-known smokers cough. I went around the rock and there was Mike setting there smoking a cigarette. He looked at me and I walked to him. We hugged as tears rolled down my cheeks. The trail I came up was the same trail I had used three times before. I was totally confused. My body was still in shock. Mike took me down to the trailhead. Gordon, Mike and I were very excited about my return. I changed clothes, drank some water and ate a sandwich. I told them what had happened and about my nightly adventure. They said they had honked the horn for me. They were thinking about going for the forest ranger for help. They were scared that a bear might have gotten me.

After our reunion, I left to get the rancher. They went back done to guard the moose. When I got to the ranch, the rancher was there. I told him that I was there yesterday. He asked if I remembered he told me that he would be across the highway cutting wood if he wasn't home. No, I did not remember. But it didn't take us long to get his horses loaded. We reached the trailhead and unloaded the horses. We put the meat packing packs on the horses and once more I headed now the trail to Arizona Lake. We had no trouble getting to the downed moose. I'm sure I couldn't convince my ankle of the no trouble part. We loaded the meat into the bags and out we came. I started out packing the antlers on my back. But after a short period, we put the rack on the horse. The extra weight was too much for my ankle.

After arriving at the trailhead, we unloaded the moose into the back of the pickup. We put a tarp under the moose meat, so it would not feel the heat of the metal truck bed. The rancher loaded his horses. I paid and thanked him for his help. We got everything situated and headed out for home. We stopped at the convenience store and bought all the ice they had. We wanted to keep the meat cool as we traveled home. I started driving home and after a short time, Mike asked me if I wanted him to drive. I asked him why. He said I was not staying on my side of the road. I pulled over and Mike drove from there. Shortly my eyes started to itch, I put my finger up to scratch it. When I took off my glasses, I found out that I was missing a lens. Therefore, I knew two things that got left down somewhere in the willows. My lens from the glasses and my wonderful old time five-gallon hat. But I brought away from the willows some great tasting moose steaks and some memories I will never forget.

YOU CAUGHT MY FISH

It was a nice warm sunny day of at least 20 degrees out on the iced over lake. It was ice fishing season in northern Wyoming. At least the wind was not howling. The temperature can be cold if the wind behaves itself. I was fishing on upper Sunshine Lake. This is my favorite lake to fish (and many others) in the winter or summer.

The fishing was slow as everyone was waiting for another school of fish to move through the area. It seemed like every fifteen to twenty minutes the poles started fluctuating up and down to show that more fish were in the area. A guy fishing about twenty feet from me had a bite. His pole tip was dancing. I watched as he hustled over to the hole in the ice. The fellow reached down and picked up the pole and gave one of those gigantic heaves as to uncover the water of its ice blanket. Snap went the line and he reeled in a line with no hook or fish.

The three of us watching couldn't resist a little giggling and teasing the fellow about his excitement and his enormous effort at setting the hook. The man took the vocal remarks in a good humorous manner. He was grumbling under his breath as he put another jig on the end of his line. He stated that he had lost his favorite red-haired jig.

A very short time later my pole started giving the bite signal.

The gentleman looked at me and stated, "Sure, you just caught my fish."

We all laughed as we had heard that statement many times before over fishing years. I carefully set the hook on my unsuspecting fish and the fight was on. I could tell the fish was one of the bigger fish in the lake by his efforts to stay away from the opening in the ice. I soon worked the fish to ease his head up through the ice passage way. With a little more effort, the fish was pulled up through the hole in the ice and deposited by my feet.

To my surprise, the fish had a red-tailed jig hooked in the corner of its mouth. Of course, we all started laughing as I did catch the other man's fish. I gave him back his jig, but the twenty-one-inch fish went home with me.

A FISHY FAN

It was a nice, but cold day on the upper Sunshine Reservoir west of Meeteetse, Wyoming. The sky was clear and the wind was calm, which made it a good day to fish through the ice. Although it was only 10 degrees, there were several fishermen spread out over the lake trying their hand at catching some of the Yellowstone Cutthroat trout. These fish are very sweet and tasty. I unloaded my ice fishing gear and ice auger on a sled and headed thirty steps out from the bank. This was a spot I had fished several times in the past. I've had good luck in this area over the years.

Arriving at the designated spot, I used the gas-powered auger to drill three holes in the ice. Two holes for fishing and one to place my stringer down into with the fish I catch to keep them fresh. After getting my lines in the water, I looked around to see if any other holes had been drilled in this area recently. There were a few holes that had been refrozen over, thus someone had been in the area the day before. Another sign was the frozen entrails of fish lying on the ice about twenty feet away.

I had caught a couple keepers. The fish were about seventeen or eighteen inches long. While I was sitting on my chair waiting for another fish to bite, I happened to see a bald eagle fly over my head. I have seen bald eagles often at this lake in the summer and also in the winter months. I watched the eagle swoop down and try to pick up the frozen entrails that were stuck to the ice. It was awesome to see the wings spread and the talons stretched out as the eagle lowered itself to pick up the fish entrails. The eagle was unable to pull the fish guts from the ice. After the eagle flew away, I went over to the frozen entrails and kicked them loose. I then threw them about twenty feet behind me on the ice.

After a couple more fish sacrificed themselves to my stringer, I heard a click-clicking sound behind me. I turned around to see what was making the noise. I was surprised to see the bald eagle walking towards the entrails on the ice. He made a short glance at me and then walked over to the entrails, took a couple pecks at them and then hooked on to them with his talons and off he flew towards the mountains. I've seen them fly that direction several times before.

The next summer, I was trolling on the lake when I headed towards a thirty-foot-high bluff on the southeast corner of the reservoir. Two bald eagles were perched at the top of the bluff. I was watching them through my binoculars. When I was within sixty yards of the bluff, one of the eagles swooped down and picked up a fish out of the water. Another wonderful act to watch in Mother Nature land. A couple weeks after that incredible sight, I saw another eagle snatch a wounded fish off the surface of the water. These are mind pleasing sights as I got to watch bald eagles in the wild do their thing. A wonderful side effect of fishing the two Sunshine Reservoirs. These fisheries are my favorite as they are taken very good care of by the Wyoming Fish and Game Department.

WELL-HELLO

A couple years ago, I took up prospecting as a hobby. Prospecting allows me to get out and enjoy nature. This is something I have been dedicated to since I was a very young boy. Watching nature at work has created many fond memories as I have enjoyed the flora and fauna of the different environments I become associated with.

I was working in the Big Horn Mountains in north-central Wyoming. While panning some gravel out of the small creek bed, I heard a loud rumbling noise behind me. I was sure it was coming from the top of the hillside that rose around fifty-feet high to the west of me. As I turned around to identify what was making the loud noise, I spotted a herd of elk moving over the top of the hill and they were headed in my direction rapidly for a cool drink of water.

The fifty or so elk herd saw me and put on their brakes. They made a right turn and headed upstream through the small valley and over the next rise in terrain. Again, I was fortunate to be a witness to Mother Nature at her best. I will never forget the sight of all those elk moving towards me. I'm sure they were amazed at the size of my eyes as I looked at them.

Another nice episode happened when I was dredging with my gold-partner in a small creek in the Big Horn Mountains. In fact, we had two dredges going. The dredge I was working on broke down. My friend Eric said I could work his deep hole with his dredge while my partner Doug and he worked on the other dredge. I gladly said, "yes" as he had air hooked up to his dredge.

This allowed me to just use goggles and not snorkel. I was down about three feet in the water laying out working the nozzle of the suction hose, when I looked up directly in front of me. An eight-inch brook trout was staring me in the eyes. We looked at each other for several minutes. I was surprised that he was not scared of me. Of course, now I was down in his own environment and besides I was loosening and turning over rock that may have larva on them which he could use for a snack. Several other smaller fish also came to check me out while I was sucking up the rock and concentrate up to the dredge. But it did not last long enough as I had to go back to my original dredge and assist my friend Doug as he got to run the nozzle and I was the helper.

Another time, Doug and I were in a different larger creek dredging. While I was under water running the nozzle, an eighteen-inch German brown trout was laying along my side waiting for his snack for the day. As I turned over the rocks and threw the larger rocks out of the way of the nozzle, the fish was waiting for larva to wash off the rocks and float to his hungry mouth. Later in the day, a special activity took place. I was busy running the nozzle under the water when Doug patted my back. I surfaced and asked him what was going on. He told me to look at the sluice box on the dredge. I took my goggles off and looked over at the sluice box. Then I saw what he was laughing at. A muskrat was digging the rocks on the sluice box. He was after the larva that was on the rocks or floating free in the water. Doug took pictures and made a short movie on his phone of our friendly little visitor. I appreciate the adventures Mother Nature presents us with in her charming ways. Many other experiences have been associated with prospecting and mining for gold. I have had fish swim up my sluice box while it was embedded in the stream bed. Ducks and geese have landed in the stream close to where I was working in the water.

FRIENDLY MINK

While fishing the Big Horn River between Thermopolis and Worland, Wyoming, I have had many mink sightings. They always seem to be friendly and not really scared of me as I observe them. Maybe they know that I don't trap wild animals. I do really like to seek them out and observe their actions. I'm sure this thinking helped trigger my interest of getting a degree in biology and teaching high school and middle school science for thirty-seven years.

My favorite mink story happened when I was bank fishing below Boysen Dam. The dam backs up water from the Wind River which flows from the Yellowstone country to Thermopolis. It was a nice warm day as I caught and released some rainbow trout and kept some walleye pike and a ling. It was one of those days when the fish were cooperating and I was enjoying myself immensely. Of course, as they say, fishing is always good and sometimes you even catch some fish. The sun shining down caused my body to want to go in nap mode. Suddenly, a rustling noise came from behind me. The wind was not blowing, so I was curious of what could be making that sound.

I turned around slowly and searched the area with my eyes looking for the source of the noise. There are several animals around this area, I did not want it to be. Animals such as snakes (rattle or otherwise), skunks, etc. Then I saw movement. The mink was rolling a pop can left by someone else. His black coat and sparkling eyes made him very attractive. Evidently, he was trying to get to some of the sweet liquid left inside. I really try to empress on my kids to take everything out with you that you brought in. Also take out what some-one else might have left. Let's help keep our country looking pristine and clear from litter.

It was fun watching the mink in action. He seemed quite concerned with the can. His feet were busy turning the can as his mouth lapped at the soda. After a couple minutes, the mink saw me. He stopped his assault on the can and looked at me as if he was a kid that got caught with his hand in the cookie jar. After a short observance, he turned and scooted between some large rocks. I watched to see what he did from there. After a couple minutes, I saw him moving along the side of the hill towards a couple of trees. He probably had a den nearby.

As I turned around to look at my poles, one had its tip bouncing up and down. Well, back to fishing.

COPPER LAKES TRIP

Our crew decided to take a fishing trip to the Copper Lakes located northwest of Cody, Wyoming. The lakes are high altitude lakes containing California golden rainbow trout. These trout need cold water to survive. Colder water contains more oxygen which these trout require. The water from the melting of glaciers and snow fields creates a nice environment for the trout.

They were shutting down the rig for a week before starting to drill another well. It was close to the fourth of July, so it would be a nice holiday fishing trip. We arranged to borrow a driller. The three of us were excited to make this trip. We made plans, collected fishing and camping supplies days before the rig shut down.

The off day finally arrived. Frank, Bill, and I loaded the horses into the trailer and filled the back of the pickup with gear as if we were going to spend three weeks instead of three days on the fishing trip. We even included a three-man rubber raft. Believe me, we had plenty of food and fishing supplies to last for our trip.

None of us had been to the lakes before. We did have a good map indicating the roads to take. We started out going up the Chief Joseph highway. This starts from about twenty miles north of Cody and goes up into the Beartooth Mountains towards Cooke City, Montana and comes back down into Red Lodge, Montana. This is a must drive for anyone looking for scenic outdoor environment. It has been listed in many magazines as one of the most wonderful pathways to travel in the summer. Turning off the main highway, we headed back southeast and climbed in elevation to the Copper Lakes trailhead. We saw several species of animals on the way up to the trailhead. Deer, antelope, elk, and even a timber rattlesnake waved as we moved up the mountain.

Once we reached the trailhead, we unloaded the horses and prepared them for the trip up the mountain. The view and smell of the region really got us excited to head up the trail. However, the sign warning us that we were in grizzly country made us look around for signs that grizzlies had frequented this area lately. Our horses did not indicate such. Horses usually can smell or sense their presence. We decided to use the young horse as the pack horse. Only one of the horses had any real experience in the mountains. The rest were flatlanders. We loaded up the young horse with our supplies. She seemed to accept the job of slave well. Then we saddled the other three horses and checked everything twice. The narrow trail leading up the mountain looked well used, so we were anxious to get started.

It looked like it was going to be a nice warm day and the sky was clear as we started up the trail. We good see the gray granite, steep-walled mountain at the very top of the skyline. It was time to catch some of those beautiful trout. As we moved up the mountain, Bill was leading the pack horse. We came to a very sharp turn in the path. The young horse became confused as if it was supposed to go around the curve or climb up the steep ground straight in front of it. Bill, not thinking of the horse's innocence, tried to bully the horse around the corner or to jump up the hill. The young horse panicked and reared up high and pulled the rope from the hand of Bill and fell over backwards down the mountain side. It was not a good sight as we watched the horse slide down the three hundred yards to the bottom of the mountain into the dry gulley below. From where we were perched, it looked like the sorrel horse might have been killed. She was not moving. We hurried down the mountain and rushed over to the colt. As we got near her, we could tell that she was just knocked out. We started to unpack the horse as she was now conscious, but scared. We looked closely at her physical condition. It was not bad for the tumble she had taken. A few minor cuts and I'm sure some bruises.

The horse stood up and looked at us like, "What are you going to do now?" We loaded the material on my horse and started back up the mountain. The young horse yelled a few times and started following us the trail. We were about three-quarters up the mountain when we found a snow field in front of us. It did not look like there was any way to go around the snow field. The field was about sixty-yards across. It did not look very deep as we made the decision to lead our horses across the snow field. Slowly, I grabbed the reins of my horse and started leading her across the patch of snow. I was about half-way across when the horse stepped up to her belly in the snow. She did not panic and made it across the field.

Frank was next with his horse. Everything was going good until his horse hit the deep spot. When it sunk up to its belly, it panicked, reared up and rolled sideways. Not good! The horse started to slide down the mountain side as if it was on a ski jump runway. I was just hoping it would stop before it hit the end. There was about a five hundred foot drop off at the end. Just at the bottom of the steepest part of the side, the horse flipped up on all four legs. From where we were standing, we could see red blood spots on her side. We were upset that she might be hurt bad.

Now, I decided it was time to head back down the mountain. Bill's horse was standing like she was set in cement. She said she was not going anywhere. So yes, it was time to return to the trailhead. Things were not going well for us. I went and got my horse and started leading her back across the snow field. We were just barely on the snow when my horse sunk into the snow and did her imitation of the other horse. She rolled over and slid down the side of the mountain. The supplies were being thrown all over the mountain as the horse slid and rolled down the snow field. This did not look good at all. My horse was not out in the open snow face. It was being slammed against rocks and trees as it continued down the edge of the snow field. The horse finally came to a stop. It was wedged between some trees.

I started down the snow field with a very negative view of what I was going to find. As I got to the horse, I saw no reaction from her. This was not good! All I could think of was what am I going to tell my brother-in-law about his horses. He would not be a happy camper. I circled around the horse and tried to untangle her legs and head from the trees. Frank came down and gave me his pistol. He said we would shoot the horse and leave it for bear food. Wow! I was not ready for that decision. I continued to work with the horse. Then I saw it wink at me. I kept moving her legs and head. She finally started kicking and finally wormed her way out from between the trees. The horse stood up on all four legs and looked over at the other horse that was standing down at the bottom of the snow field. To think that I almost shot the horse at several times as I was trying to get her free from the trees.

We did not worry about getting the stuff off the snow field as the poles were broken and the raft was torn. All we could think of was to get the horses off the mountain and back to the trailhead camp area. I led my horse down to the other horse standing on the snow field. From there, we moved all the horses back down the trail. After getting back to the pickup, we checked all the horses for damage. I was relieved to find out that none of the horses were badly hurt. In fact, my horse probably had fewer cuts on it then the other horses. We petted and rubbed the horses until they were all settled down.

We were standing there talking about our ordeal when we saw three guys walking down the trail towards us. When they got to us, they asked us if we were going to go up to the lakes fishing. We told them not now. They said it was a good thing as the lakes were still frozen over with a thick sheet of ice. Oh wow, what else could go wrong? I'm sorry I asked. On the way out, we had a flat tire on the trailer. We had to unhook the trailer and take off the tire. You got it. No spare. I stayed with the horses as they took the tire to Cody to get fixed.

When we finally got the horses back to my brother-in-law's place, he took the news well. We doctored the horses and told him all about our adventure. I'm glad he had a good sense of humor.

THE FISH DANCE

I was going to take Raena, my fishing buddy fishing. My six-year-old granddaughter was very anxious for tomorrow to show up. It was early spring. The spawning trout were starting to come in to the bay by the boat dock at a local lake. The trout being released from that area several years before tend to return to the area of release to lay their eggs. The shoreline is usually filled with many fishermen. Most of the people fishing are catching and releasing the fish back into the water.

The evening before the trip to the lake, I entered Raena's bedroom to tell her the nightly bedtime story. I asked her what topic she wanted to hear a story about. She responded that a fishing story would be nice. It was the choice I wanted, I knew if my granddaughter did catch a big fish, she would want to bring it home to show everyone.

I told Raena about a grandfather taking a little girl to the lake fishing. The little girl caught a big fish. The young girl was so excited when she caught the big fish that she couldn't wait to get it home to show her grandmother her big fish. However, her grandfather told her that maybe they should put the fish back into the lake. The little girl frowned and said she wanted to take it home. The grandfather told her how he thought the fish would miss all her friends in the lake. The fish would be sad to leave its home and would miss living with its fish friends, turtles and snakes. He told her how it was common to release the fish back into the water. Then the person would do a fish dance as she thanked the fish for letting her catch it and while she wished it a nice day. Therefore, the little girl and the fish would be happy.

The next morning, we walked out of the house with our fishing poles and a couple dozen night crawler worms. The sixty-mile drive was quite eventful as we saw several nice mule deer bucks and a couple pheasants. We talked about how our ice fishing was fun during the winter. Yes, Raena was my fishing buddy.

When we reached the lake, I parked above the bay. We were both excited to catch some fish. The weather was warm as the blue sky with small cotton clouds welcomed us to the day. The light orange sun furnished us with warm rays. We walked done to the edge of the lake and found a spot between a couple fisherman. It was interesting to see how different people were attempting to catch the spawning fish as they moved through the bay. Some fly fishermen were using different techniques to attract the fish. A couple fishermen were in float tubes further out in the bay. Raena and I were going to use the original fish mainstay. What fish can resist an earthworm?

It was my granddaughter's job to pick out the lucky worm to place on the hook. She gave me the worm and I dressed the hook. After placing worms on both poles, I casted the lines out being careful not to interfere with any other lines. Then we set down to wait patiently for a bite. Raena waited for a short time and then got up and went looking for pretty rocks.

Then I noticed a small bobbing of the tip on her pole. I told Raena that she might have a bite. By the time she got to her pole, the tip took to bouncing up and down. Having learned how to set a hook from previous fishing trips, she pulled up on the pole and the fight was on, I could tell by the pressure on the line that she had a nice fish hooked. I told her to tighten the drag a little. Raena turned the dial a little and continued to reel the fish in. People were watching as my granddaughter fought the fish. She was starting to tire as the fish was not happy having the hook in its lip.

She asked me to take over while she rested. I took the pole and just held it for a short time and then gave it back to Raena. She finished reeling the fish up to the shoreline. Then she backed up and brought the flopping three or four pound fish on the bank. She came up to help me grab the fish. I unhooked the fish. I asked her if it was okay to place the fish back into the water. She smiled and helped me place the fish into the lake. After we watched the fish power its tail and swim out into the water, I turned to pick up the pole. As I turned around, I saw Raena dancing and yelling her thanks to the fish for letting her catch it. She told the fish she was happy for it to get back in the water with its friends and she hoped it had a good day. A large smile came over my face and my love and affection for my granddaughter climbed another notch. That was the only fish we caught that day. We went to the picnic table later and had a nice lunch as we roasted hot dogs and toasted marshmallows for dessert.

YEP! I SAW ONE

My senior year in high school was a good year. Many fond memories were created by school activities, but one of the events that stood out above all the others happened during deer hunting season. I lived about four miles south of town on a farm/ranch. There were two different watershed areas close to my home. These created a variety of entertainment for me over the years. Like Tom Sawyer and Huck Finn, I was able to roam the watershed flood plains and live among Mother Nature and her wonderful existence.

During deer hunting season (1964), I was hunting along the banks of the Shoshoni River which flows from Cody to Lovell, Wyoming. It passes right below the elevated town of Byron. Between the old dirt road that goes across the river bridge over the Shoshoni river and was an ideal deer hunting area. The flood plain along the river was bordered by an alfalfa field and a region of willows, marsh and prairie desert. All this flora produced a good feeding and hiding place for mule deer.

On this nice October day, I was moving through the vegetation looking for a big buck to fill out my hunting license. As it turned out, I did wound a deer and was in quick pursuit of the deer when I came around some tall willows and froze in my tracks. There snarling at me with "all the better to eat you with" teeth was a wolf. Yes, a real live mean-looking wolf. I had never seen a wolf before. They were not supposed to be around this area, especially not this far from Yellowstone Park. This was thirty years before the wolves were reintroduced to the park. The wolf was saying the downed buck was his. Who was I to argue? It was time to do "exit stage right". I left the region quickly and hurried home to tell anyone who would listen what had happened.

My family laughed at me fearing a coyote. My friends in school on Monday made laughter at my run in with a coyote. Coyotes are small and usually quite timid. The large snarling animal was a wolf. I had seen many coyotes over the years. A week later, a couple friends of mine came to school very excited and agreed with me that indeed there was a wolf wandering the flood plain of the river just below the town of Byron. Another adventure in the wild was proven true. I have never heard of another wolf being spotted that low in altitude or around the Byron area. In a way, I was very lucky to have the opportunity to see the wolf. However, at the time, I was quite frightened by the snarling teeth and the not so friendly attitude of the wolf. That mouth of teeth will always reside in my mind.

The year before I fortunate to see a lynx about two miles upstream from where I saw the wolf. Another animal that was not supposed to be found in our lower elevation. She was a very splendid looking animal. I felt very lucky to witness the appearance of both animals in the wild.

THEY KNOW!

I love nice fall days that are warm and have clear skies. But this weekend, I wish it was cooler. I'm elk hunting on Green Mountain in west central Wyoming. The opening day of the season is the first of October. It should not be eighty degrees on top of this mountain. But I guess it is better than a snow blizzard and freezing temperatures. Green Mountain is a pine tree covered mountain in the middle of a semi-arid temperate desert. An oasis for animals in the area. Deer, elk, and even a large herd of wild horses frequent this area for food, water, and shelter.

The last couple years, I have had good luck with filling my cow elk tag. The trouble is when it is warm, you have the problem of getting the delicious meat home without it getting too hot and rotting. After losing the first elk I got from this area, I learned to bring a lot of chunk ice with me. This would get me to a town where I could get more ice to make it the hundred miles to the meat processor.

Today, it is going to be in the high seventies or low eighties. I descended from the south-facing mountain side looking for a good used game trail. As luck was with me, I found a spot where three trails intersected. A tall pine tree beckoned me. After crawling up the tree, I nestled in on a good branch location that allowed me to observe the trails coming up from the magnificent Red Desert to the south.

As noon approached, the sun had me wrapped in a nice warm blanket and my eyelids wanted to check for leaks. They kept closing and sure enough, all was well as they blocked out the bright sun from my eyes. I was just so relaxed and feeling nice and cozy when a large bull elk came up under my tree and bugled. Not a soft grunt, but a loud spine jingling, ear popping bugle that sent startled nerve messages throughout my body. I almost dropped my rifle and fell out of the tree. I looked down at the old white-gray bodied elk. He looked up at me with his huge antlers pointed back and his eyes sparkling with mischief and bugled again. He was having fun at my expense. Again, he gave me that ha-ha gotcha look and turn and started to walk away. I swear he was prancing as he left laughing. I'm sure he had played his tom-foolery on many unsuspecting hunters that had cow permits. The bull elk walked about forty feet away and looked back and did another bugle laugh and walked off into the trees.

I climbed down out of the tree. I decided to follow a trail that traveled along the side of the mountain towards an area that I knew a spring came out of the side of the mountain. Maybe some cow elk would be there drinking the cool clear spring water. As I came around some trees, I saw a golden eagle hopping around on the ground. I could see a pile of entrails left by some hunter who had luck in getting his elk. It was funny because the eagle had eaten so much that he was having a hard time getting air born. He stood by his food pile and let me move on by. I continued along the trail and rounded a tight group of trees out into a small treeless opening covered by grass and sagebrush. Standing in the middle of the open area was another large bull elk. The elk did not seem to be very friendly. He started pawing at the ground and flipping dirt with his large antlers. I'm sure he was hinting for me to move along. He did not have to signal many more times as I was glad to move on to another trail that was going in the direction I wanted to go. Man, two large bulls at very close range and I have a cow tag. They knew, I tell you. They knew that I had a cow permit and they just made fun of me, I'm sure they were a hit that night at their gatherings as they told how they had fun with this hunter who dared enter their turf. I got my cow the next day. However, the most pleasant memories of that hunting trip were the actions of the two-bull elk that enjoyed themselves as they entertained themselves at my expense.

NOT AS WISE AS AN OWL

In the summer of 1963, I was sophomore in high school. I had learned a lot in the classroom and from the many different sports I played. But on this nice warm summer day, I was taught a new lesson.

After walking two miles to get to the Coon Creek drainage area, I headed to the group of Russian olive trees that existed on the flood plain. I really liked the environment that this flood plain produced as it was an oasis in the middle of a semi-arid temperate desert. The creek meandered through sand hills covered with sparse grass, sagebrush, cactus, yucca, and greasewood plants. A wide variety of fauna used the flood plain region as a place to find food, water and homes. I called this grouping of Russian olive trees, Owl Town. There were several great-horned owl nests located in the top of the trees.

Most of the time, I laid on the top of a hill close by and observed the animals as they did their everyday routines. I knew that there were baby owls in a couple of the nest. I had seen them with my binoculars from the hill on other days. Today, I wanted to climb up the tree and look in the nest. It would be cool to see the baby owls up close.

As I walked along the base of the hill towards the nests through the high knee-high grass, I saw a fifty-five-gallon barrel lid lying at a high angle in the grass. Like any young boy, I decided I would step on the lid and smash it down in the grass. I stepped on the lid. To my surprise, my foot moved and I almost fell down as my balance was altered. I looked down at the lid and a porcupine waddled out from under the lid. Yes, it startled me quite a bit. But it was also funny as the porcupine moved along as if he had been awakened from his comfortable nap. I'm sure he was annoyed and upset that I had disrupted his nap. He slowly walked off into the high grass and disappeared.

I continued to walk towards Owl Town. I was getting anxious to see the baby owls. They were still in their white fluff. When I reached the base of one of the trees that contained a nest, I looked around and did not see any adult owls around. I climbed up through the thorny branches to get to the nest. Up I climbed. The thorns poked at my hands and tried to tear my leather coat that I wore to help protect me from them. I was almost to the nest when I heard a screech and saw a shadow above my head. Then I saw the large great-horned owl swooping towards my right shoulder. I swear the talons were big enough to block out the sun. The owl swept by me and barely missed contacting my coat. The owl turned around and was coming back for another try. I was convinced that it was time to get down out of the tree as soon as possible. The thorns tried to help the owl in convincing me that climbing Russian olive trees was not a good idea. I made it to the bottom as the owl landed in the top of the tree. My hands were scratched and bleeding a little. My coat had some puncture marks, but I was okay. I know now that it was not a good decision to have a close encounter with the baby owls. I'll observe from the hill side from a distance.

Across from where I was standing is a vertical hill side rising about 200 feet straight up. On the side of the hill is a wind cut out which contains a golden eagle nest. I wonder if I could repel down and get a good look at the baby eagles. No! I tell myself. That would not probably be a good idea.

GETTING AFTER THE GOLD

I had just got started in my new hobby of prospecting and mining for gold. A new club was starting in Worland, Wyoming. Worland is in the Big Horn Basin. This means mountains and streams abound in any direction. A good place to launch from to search for some gold flakes.

At the first meeting I went to, I was introduced to Doug. Come to find out, he was raised in the same town in Alaska as Parker and his grandfather (Haines). However, Doug informed me that all he wanted to do as a young man was to fish and hunt. Now the streams he frequented are shown on tv to have gold deposits. Doug has had several years of prospecting experience since he came down to the lower forty-eight states. I was all ears and quickened heart beats as we discussed prospecting. I explained that I found some small flakes in a spot out in the badlands. The spot I found lacked water for panning. This created a problem of transporting the classified gravel.

Doug and the gold club talked about a creek about eight-five miles away. They talked about how you were assured to find and process gold flakes. The flakes were very small but in abundance. Doug and I decided to take his dredge up to the creek and he would show me the process involved in dredging for gold. It was May and the water coming off the nearby mountains would still be cool. But we were hooked. I especially wanted to try my luck at working the nozzle of the dredge hose. Doug asked me if I had a wet suit. I informed him that I did not have one although I had an idea of how to help make my body warm enough to be in the water. Okay, so I had gold fever. I was going to make the effort no matter what. Doug said his wet suit must have shrunk since the last time he was in the water. One must be careful of how he lays it out to dry. I just smiled and expressed my wonderment about maybe a little weight gain may have also played a part.

My idea was to wear a rain suit next to my skin. Then I would wear sweats and also wear a rain suit over my sweats. Two pair of socks and snow packs hopefully will keep my feet warm. A stocking cap under the rain coat hood tied down tight should protect my head. Two pairs of waterproof gloves would protect my hands. Wearing all this garb, I helped unload the dredge and we pulled up stream where we decided to dredge a back-whirl area in the stream. I wish the water flow was less, but oh well! After anchoring the dredge and leveling the sluice box where Doug figured we had the best chance of collecting the fine gold flakes, we started up the engine. Doug explained how I was to work the nozzle as not to plug it up. The three-inch opening could plug up with rocks too big to enter the nozzle or too much sand at once could cause a plug up in the hose. I was anxious to get started although I could feel the coolness of the water already chilling my body. But it wasn't too bad to stop me from trying to dredge.

It was time to get after it. The water depth was only around eighteen inches and I kneeled and started to let the nozzle suck up the sand. Of course, I got in a hurry and plugged up the hose a few times. Doug counselled me on how to be more efficient, so we would run more material over the sluice box at an even pace. Things were going good except the hole was getting deeper where I was working. This meant that I was getting more submerged in the water. As more total body was under water, the cooler my body became. I managed to work for four hours in the stream then my body started the shivers and shaking. I could tell that I was getting too cold. My body temperature was cooling down. The thought of hyperthermia was entering my mind. We decided it was time to pull the dredge back down stream and do a cleanup of the mats to pan some of the concentrate to see how we did.

I was for changing into dry clothes and then help with the clean-up then helping to load up the dredge back on my pickup bed. So, while Doug took the mats off the sluice box and washed them off in a five-gallon bucket, I went and changed. The mats did contain about twenty to twenty-five thousand small flakes of gold. That really sounds like a lot of gold. However, the flakes are so small that it takes about two hundred and fifty thousand flakes to make an ounce of gold.

I really did enjoy my first attempt at dredging. I have dredged many times over the last four years. Right after that first time, I ordered a cold-water wet suit, gloves, and snorkel/goggles. Even with the 7mm wet suit, the water can be quite chilly at times. We are working to get warm water hooked up to the dredge to pump into our suits. Boy, that would make a difference for sure. I only wish I would have gotten involved in prospecting at a much younger age. Say thirties, not sixties.

I LIKE DEER

Over the years, I have had some unique experiences with mule or white-tail deer. When I was in high school, I was riding my horse along the top of a hill over-looking the three beaver ponds which I really like to observe the wild-life. As I approached the edge of the hill, I heard a noise which sounded like something coming up the side of the hill. Bang! I was right. A large mule deer buck came charging up over the hill and placed its shoulder against my horse's shoulder. All three of us were shocked at the presence of each other and the accidental contact. As I was riding bareback, the sudden movement of my horse almost caused me to fall off the horse.

The deer did not stick around to apologize for his improper abuse to my horse. If I had my refereeing license, I would have thrown my flag for unnec-essary roughness. Since the buck was a five point and had such a large body, I followed it down off the hill and saw it go into a patch of willows. I knew that group of willows well, as I played in it a lot over the years. I knew that there was a small grassy area in the middle of the willows that made a good hide-out for me as a youngster and also a good spot for the deer to hide, graze, and sleep.

I tethered my horse and walked the game trail into the willows. I wanted another look at the buck at close range. But not as close as last time. After I had just entered the willows, several does come running up the trail towards me. I had to take a nose-dive into the willows or get run over by the charging hooves. Alright, I get the message. It was time to go get my horse and head back towards the beaver ponds. I really don't think that buck sent those does to deter me from catching up with him. But after all, it is hunting season and he was a smart enough to live this long. I wonder, no I doubt it; but maybe.

Another time, I was hunting with some friends in eastern Montana. A couple of my football player's fathers wanted to take me hunting deer on one of their ranches. Who am I to resist the offer? I liked to hunt back then and I knew that they would put me in a good position to fill my tag. I like wild game meat. The three of us spread out and were walking across a prairie pasture that did not have any cattle on it at this time.

As we made our way through the middle of the pasture, we came to an area that was full of red rag weed. The weeds were about three feet high. The fellows motioned to me to be on the lookout for deer as they could lay down and hide in the weeds. It so happened at the time, I was standing on a small uprising in the field. Several yards in front of me, I saw the weeds moving. On a closer look, I could make out a white-tailed buck low-crawling through the weeds. I had never seen a deer crawl on its knees through covering brush or weeds before. I was amazed as the four-point buck continued to scoot through the weeds. The problem for him was the weed patch was coming to an end. Even though the buck ate grass and weeds, he was good tasting.

One of my favorite incidents occurred when I was sitting on the bank of a river fishing. I had fished this hole several times in the past. I was in a secluded spot back off from the country road. Willows, weeds and high grass hid me from road traffic. It was a nice warm fall day and I was having some good luck catching and releasing some nice rainbow and brown trout. I was enjoying the quiet (except flora and fauna natural sounds) and good scenery. The moving water did sound good as it reminded me of memories of being a frontiersman as a young boy exploring, camping and fishing the creek and its flood plain. I have always liked the sound of water moving in a creek or river, especially towards late afternoon or early evening.

All of a sudden, my attention was attracted to some noise behind me. It sounded like something was there. But what something was entering my mind. I turned around and saw a fine looking four-point white-tailed buck looking at me as if he did not like my presence. He was stomping his hoof on the ground, blowing a little snot out his nose and letting me know I was in his territory. It was fun watching him warn me to move along. When he started to throw some dirt with his antlers, I knew he meant business. I didn't know if I wanted to laugh or throw rocks at him. Although, if he did decide to attack, my only escape was to jump in the river. I've waded that area before, so that didn't bother me too much. Finally, the buck figured I got the message and turned around and went into a group of willows not far away. I continued to fish for a couple more hours.

A few weeks later, I went back to the same area to fish. You got it. The buck showed up again. Only this time he brought his twin brother with him. Now there were two hands me. They both looked troubled over me being located in their neck of the woods. They did not put on the three-act play to chase me away, but they did snot a little which I took as a negative gesture. They turned and walked off cussing me I'm sure, I fished that spot several times in my later years. But did not see my friends again. I did have a beaver bang his tail on the water telling me to try a different spot. I just believe the habitat area was special to many animals; including me.

When I was going to college at Rocky Mountain College in Billings, Montana, a friend of mine asked me to go on a fishing trip with him and another friend of his. Well, I was kind of busy until he said we were going after California golden rainbow trout towards the top of the m Billings. Golden rainbows are high altitude fish. They like cold clear water because of the higher oxygen content. They think glacier lakes are their resort palaces. Now the trip was becoming a great idea. Could already imagine the scenery and what wildlife we might come across in ascending the mountain.

The nature gods were kind to us as the day arrived for us to leave. The sky was clear and ideal weather was being predicted for the day. I was pumped and ready when they picked me up in their college pickup. I was assured that it would get us there and back. It's not the exterior looks, but the interior shape that counts. The vehicle ran like a charmed machine and all doubt was washed out of my mind. As we moved higher in elevation, the semi-level farm/ranch land gave way to heavier wooded rougher terrain. We followed a small creek up into glacial cut-out canyon to East Rosebud Lake. The coniferous trees joined the other flora to produce a green background for us to view the many fig-saw puzzle scenes as we continued to the trailhead. Once we reached the trailhead, I was surprised to see very few vehicles in the parking area. All the better for us to make the climb up the mountain without much disturbance of noise and other human interference. From the trailhead, several different trails could be taken.

Most of the trails were shorter and less steep than the path we were going to take. Having played football and baseball during the school year, I was still in good shape. Well, any way I was going to find out how much my legs swore at me as we climbed from six thousand feet to over nine thousand feet in elevation.

We unloaded our gear and adjusted our backpacks. It was time to start up the trail. It was a little cool so early in the morning, but I'm sure I will warm up shortly as we incline. The trail was in excellent condition. You could tell that the forest rangers and summer helpers had prepared the path for hikers or fisherman like ourselves. I was thankful for their efforts, as I have walked many a trail that was not in very good condition and created serious hazards for moving up a mountain.

Shortly, as we started our climb, a guide joined us. The large five-point mule deer buck stood on the trail in front of us. I'm sure I saw him beckon with his head for us to follow him. So, we did. He would stay about fifty-feet in front of us occasionally stopping to turn around and look to see if we were still following him. Of course, he was the source of our conversation with a mixture of the excitement of going after California Goldens. College activities and summer plans also added to our visiting as we steadily climbed up the trail. At times the deer would disappear from view, but soon he would reappear on the trail and stand there staring at us as if he figured we would give up the climb and head back down the mountain to the flatlands where humans are supposed to be located.

The buck looked elegant as he posed for us. His coat was outstanding as his brownish-tan color and large rack stood out against the green forage background and the burnt-red dirt colored trail. Of course, none of us had a camera. Why! Oh why, did I not take a serious liking for photography in my life. So many wonderful pictures could have been taken. They were taken by my eyes and stored in my brain. But it would have been nice to share the places and the many different scenes that Mother Nature has afforded me the opportunity to be a part of.

We continued our ascent until the trees started to become less abundant. We were getting above the tree-line. Smaller trees and brush became the standard flora. Then the deer disappeared as we moved out into an open area where a good-sized lake appeared nestled into the base of some very barren, jagged mountains. The glacial lake was a beautiful sight as there was no wind and the surface set still and looked like a mirror. Our excitement now was growing leaps and bounds as we were anxious to wet a line.

We threw out a wide variety of lures, spinners, and flies at the fish. I'm not sure of why they did not want to play the game. We found it very hard to catch a fish. Either they saw us and were not interested in playing our game or maybe they were spawning. Didn't they know we just wanted to have some fun with them and then return them back to the lake? We did have a couple dozen worms. Now what fish can reject an earthworm? That would be like me rejecting a hamburger of a slice of pizza. Sure enough, we did catch a few on the worms and a couple on spinners. They are definitely a beautiful fish with their reds, orange, golden-yellow colors.

I was fishing away when I heard a noise behind me. I turned around to see a marmot helping himself to my sack lunch. Now I don't mind sharing my lunch with him as long as he left me some. He liked my sandwich and left me part of my chips and candy bars. This was the first marmot that I had ever seen. They are a lot larger than a rock chuck. They look like they could be dangerous if he was cornered or upset. I slowly eased myself in his direction and he moved away towards some brush not far away. I was glad to see the animal, but my stomach was not happy at loosing part of my lunch.

The trip was one of my favorite mountain experiences. The scenery was excellent and of course the fishing was excellent also as fishing always is. Sometimes you catch fish and other times, you don't. But being out in the wild creates memories and mental photos that you will always retain. We didn't see our guide on the way down the mountain. I guess he had other appointments with other visitors of the mountains.

GREAT BLUE HERON

In my middle school years, I was fortunate to help a beautiful bird. One day as I was adjusting the water in the ditch so I could dam it up to flood irrigate the pasture, I noticed a large bird limping across the pasture. The bird looked like it had a hurt wing. In our science class, we had many bird cards which showed a picture of the bird and information about its habitat and migration patterns, if the bird did so. Our teacher quizzed us on the bird identification cards. We were tested on them with so many given each week until we learned about all the birds. I was very interested in nature and enjoyed learning about the birds. I recognized this bird from its card. It was the first time I had ever seen one in the wild. My excitement was high as I went into the house to tell my brother and folks about the bird in the pasture.

My younger brother was anxious to see the bird. Dad also came outside to look. When we went through the gate into the pasture, we saw the heron laying against the fence. He did not look very healthy, I'm sure he feared us and was unsure of his future. I asked my dad what we could do to help the heron get better. His view was to let it alone and if he was healthy enough, he would make it on his own. My brother and I was concerned that the dogs would kill it. We wanted to take care of it. After some discussion, Dad agreed to let us put it into the back room of the chicken coop. The room was not being used at this time of the year. We used the room to raise bum lambs or baby chickens.

We went and got a light blanket to throw over the bird to capture it. The blue heron was weak and never but up much of a fight as I picked it up and carried it to the room. Our excitement continued as we decided what to do next for the heron. We obtained a covered water container that we used to water the young chickens. We also placed some chicken feed in a trough for the heron, I didn't know what else to feed it. We had a heat lamp hanging in the middle of the room. We decided to turn it on for a day or so to take any chill out of the room. My brother suggested that we put a little grain in a container also in case the heron didn't like the chicken food. I agreed, and it was done.

I checked on the heron a couple times a day. I could tell that some of each of the food was gone and kept his water fresh. After three days, I opened the window and let fresh air into the room. I also felt when the heron felt well enough, it would fly out the window and return to nature.

After having the heron for a week, I was anxious for the heron to fully heal, but I also would miss it when it decided to leave. It sure looked in better shape today when I checked its food and water. It did not seem scared of us, but still didn't want to be touched. The next day when I went out to check on it, it was gone. I was excited to tell everyone that the great blue heron had flown the coop. I was happy for the heron, but also sad that it was gone. My science teacher was also my baseball coach. I kept him informed of the heron's progress and he was glad to hear that the heron did so well and returned to its natural life. The experience reinforced my love for nature.

RIVER OTTERS

One of the best organisms at playing hide-seek in the wild seems to be the river otter. Over the years of fishing, hiking and hunting, I have had the pleasure of seeing otters once. I was fishing west of Cody, Wyoming. I was fishing the north fork of the Shoshoni River. I was about half way to Yellowstone Park. Of course, Mother Nature had painted a great scene for me.

Casting my line out to a clear moving stream and enjoying the forest sounds and green floral background, my day was assured of being nothing but a success. I happened to look up just in time as a family of otters were making their way along the opposite shoreline. They were in no hurry, but they did keep moving along the edge of the rocky bank of the river. I put my pole down and tried to keep them in sight as long as I could.

They did stop for a short moment to play and splash in the calm water. But it did not last long enough as they crawled back on the bank and off they went. But I got to see a sight that not too many people get to see in the wild. I fished that area several more times over the years, but never saw the otter again. Oh darn!

HIDE MY DEER

I had heard a lot about the old gold town of Kerwin, Wyoming. It is located about twenty-five miles south-west of Meeteetse. The area was a hot bed for copper and gold prospecting. The trip was on a road that follows the Wood River flood plain. The drive is a great nature adventure. One needs a good four-wheel drive vehicle and must be aware of the weather past and present. The river could be low running water or it might be running high from rains or melt water higher up in the mountains. At several spots, you must cross the river bed over the rocks left behind from flooding in the past.

The further up the valley I travelled, the more rugged the terrain and flood plain became. At a couple places the road disappeared. It was replaced by the exposed riverbed. I had to look ahead to see where the opening in the trees ahead would indicate access back to the road. I figured if I kept to the base of the mountain to my right, I would find the road again. I was right. The scenery was great! A combination of deciduous, conifers, spruce, willows, sagebrush, and grass created a floral bouquet set forth by Mother Nature.

I finally reached the gate telling me I had reached the end of the line. The buildings from the old town still stood. A few tailing piles from mines were present on my side of the river. The large hard rock mine and many buildings were across the river. I read the nice informative messages and illustrations that have been prepared by the forest service. I was surprised to learn that Amelia Earhart was going to have a cabin built further upstream. The mining operation kept trying to make a go of it, but the ore just was not justifying the economics involved.

After exploring the area, I tried my luck at panning for gold in the river. Sorry to say that I had little success. A few very small flakes found their way into my pan. Just the thought of miners a hundred years before had prospected and mined the same spots left me smiling.

I was half way back out of the beautiful valley when a mule deer doe and young fawn crossed the road in front of me. I'm glad they far enough away that there was no chance of hitting them with my vehicle. What I saw next was another one of the wonders of nature that I so looked forward too. The doe jumped the fence along the road and the fawn crawled under the bottom wire. Then I saw the doe look at the fawn as if to say hide my baby hide. The fawn dropped down and stretched out in the high grass as its mom walked slowly away. The doe kept looking back at me as if to draw my attention away from her fawn. It was a perfect example of mother-daughter protection in the wild. I've seen birds act like they have a broken wing before as they moved away from their ground nest. These examples always leave me admiring animals and their natural instincts.

The day was a successful adventure. I hope to enjoy nature and its wonder for many years to come.

BADGERS

Badgers as I have come to adore are one of the most ferocious, adaptive hunters, and handsomest critters in Mother Nature land. Their exquisite eyes and heavy coat of grayish-brown hair with the light black stripe, not only gives them pleasant coloration, but also a good camouflage for hiding and stalking. With their strong, sharp teeth and claws, they are close to the top of the wilderness food chain. Therefore, anyone who frequents Mother Nature's playground has probably run into them or let's say saw one and gave it plenty of room to do whatever was on their agenda for the day.

I was raised on a farm/ranch in north central Wyoming. The area is a semi-arid temperate prairie-desert. Prairie dogs, mice, snakes, and such are abundant and offer a good variety for the badger's meals. The badger likes to dig burrows in the grass land or even in fields close to known prairie dog towns or other bountiful food sources. The farmers and ranchers aren't appreciative of the holes in their land as they can cause injury to livestock or cause irrigation problems.

My first run in with a badger was when I was helping my dad irrigate in a sugar beet field. We were cleaning out the start of each furrow, so the water would run smoothly down between the rows of young beet plants. From some higher grass on the ditch bank, a badger waddled out between us. I was in awe as the badger didn't seem scared of us. He acted like he owned the field. Dad and I looked at the badger and didn't know if we wanted to stay and defend our field or maybe say it was lunch time and come back at a later part of the day. The badger went into his professional fight stance and was ready to get it on. He was hissing and showing teeth as he went into his offensive mode. He pivoted as if he was on a swivel plate, as he looked at Dad and then pivoted around to snarl at me.

My dad and I both had shovels to protect ourselves. We kept moving in a very slow motion just to watch his maneuvering process. Dad was smiling as he looked at me as to see if I had wet my pants. Not yet, I thought. The badger did not act like it was going to charge, but just was going to hold us at bay. He figured we were invading his turf and it was for us to leave him alone. The badger was not a happy camper as he first snarled at my father, then at me. I have to say; the badger had my attention. After several minutes, my dad signaled me to back away and he did the same. When we finally were far enough away and out of the badger's safe space zone, he waddled off in the high grass and weeds along the ditch bank. Dad asked if I wanted to go catch the badger. No, I replied, let's finish getting these furrows cleaned out!

Dad and discussed the adventurous affair as the badger departed. He explained the to me about the badger's abilities and how he respected the animal for its intensity and fighting capabilities. To say the least, I was impressed. From then on, the badger became one of my favorite animals. I know they can be a hazard for farmers and ranchers. However, ranchers especially like the badger for its help in controlling the population of prairie dogs. The prairie dog also creates a problem because of it tunneling under the ground and the holes it makes. Horses and cows can step into the holes and break a leg. But to me, the prairie dog and badger are part of nature's plan. In fact, I pulled off to the side of the road a couple days ago. A badger was working his way down a hill side not far from a known prairie dog town. I have seen a badger just lie still in the middle of a prairie dog town and wait for one to pop up out of it hole. To observe a badger digging into the mouth of a hole to get at a prairie dog or gopher, is an exciting demonstration of power and adaptive force to get supper.

Many years later my son Lance and I were traveling to Sunshine Reservoir to go fishing. As we turned off the black top road on to a dirt/gravel road that would take us to the lake, a badger crossed in front of our vehicle.

Lance yelled, "Stop Dad, let's catch it!"

Smiling, I pulled over to the side of the road. Lance jumped out of the truck and started after the badger. I got out of the truck and followed in pursuit. When I caught up with my son, I found him in a defensive stance and not really thinking of picking up the badger any more.

The badger had stopped running and had taken up a defensive position. He was hissing and snarling at Lance. I asked Lance if he still wanted to pick up the badger. He looked at me as if I was crazy. We watched the badger's reaction to us (as I remember my dad and I doing the same thing). I mentioned to my son to back away slowly as did I, When the badger felt we far enough away, he went under the barbed wire fence and waddled out in to the rancher's grass pasture. I could see some prairied dog mounds far off in the middle of the grass pasture. My son was amazed at the actions of the badger. Every now and then over the years, the badger incident comes alive when we get together. I still can't talk him in to trying to catch a badger, what an amazing animal, I really enjoy seeing it in the wild.

Another badger encounter comes to mind when I think about an elk hunting trip I was on in the badlands. I was walking along the top of a flat-topped hill looking down at the water shed below. I was hoping that some elk would be close to the small creek meandering below me. I was really engrossed in observing what was going on in the flood plain area of the stream. There was very little water moving, but a small pool here and there was present.

As I walked the crest of the hill being careful to not step on cactus or in one of the prairie dog holes, my mind was still on the area down below. Until an object in motion was seen straight in front of me, brought my mind to other things. A badger was running straight toward me. He seemed like he was a middle linebacker heading for a sure tackle. I played middle linebacker in college. This badger was on a mission. The way this badger was coming at me, made me wonder if he was rabid, I never heard of a badger having rabies, but a lot of skunks in this area have shown signs of rabies in the past. Maybe the badger went three rounds with a rabid skunk.

Meanwhile, the badger kept making a charging motion towards me. I thought about shooting the badger. This would solve my problem with the badger, but also scare away any elk in the area. I had to make my decision pretty quick as the badger was only around twenty feet away. I noticed that I was standing in the middle of a prairie dog town. There were holes all around me. And yet, the badger was still heading at my legs as a bowling ball moving towards the pins. And the when the badger was ten feet away from me, the badger scooted down into a hole in front of me. I was glad that I did not have to shoot the animal. The little feller had put some fright in to my soul. I did not know what was on his mind.

Yes, I do have a fond respect for this animal. I have perched myself on a hill and watched them dig. Those powerful claws can rival those of a bear or wolverine for their ability to rip and tear through the soil. I was standing in the grassy prairie along the fence line I was repairing. The badger I was staring at was getting somewhat nervous as he looked at me looking at him. I was keeping my distance, so I would not disrupt his effort at digging his hole in the ground.

I took a step towards him. I know from passed experiences with badgers that they are not really aggressive in their behavior. They are basically a self-defense animal. Back me into a corner and then look out. Most animals are that way. Pressure them or threaten their offspring and then they become a world of hurt for you.

After a few minutes of mutual staring at each other, I backed away. He looked at me and walked away as if he was a strutting bandy rooster. We both were feeling good about ourselves. I really like to observe this magnificent animal any chance I get. I've seen a dozen or more over the years. It is almost like watching a cross between a bull-legged cowboy and a pit bull as the badger walks away to do his thing. Very cool!

ELK

It's a mystery why I did not go elk hunting over the years when I was younger. It was probably because I was so enthused with football and basketball when I was in high school and college. I did do some deer hunting while I was younger, but never did get a chance or even remembering if I had really wanted to hunt the larger elk. Now that I have tasted it, I would have jumped at the chance.

My first chance to go after the Wapiti was when I had returned from teaching in North Dakota and Montana. I was lucky enough to land a teaching and coaching position in my home town of Byron, Wyoming. One of the neat things about this coaching position was that my high school basketball coach was the assistant football coach when I was in high school and now, he was my assistant football coach. I was pleased to have Bob Dorr as my assistant. I had always respected him for his beliefs and personality. A fine man indeed.

I'm thirty-five now and my brother-in-law has asked me to go elk hunting with him. We both applied for an elk hunting license (permit) and we both drew a bull tag. To say I was excited would be an understatement. My first elk hunting trip should be very exciting. Our hunting permit area was for the Sunlight Creek region. This was a very beautiful mountainous area which was in Sunlight Basin. This area was not new to me. The Chief Joseph Highway now runs through this region. It is one of the most intriguing drives around as it goes from north of Cody, Wyoming up through the Beartooth Mountains to Cooke City, Montana back down the mountain via a long looping, switchbacks to Red Lodge, Montana have driven the highway many times. The problem was at the time of the hunting trip, the road was a dirt/gravel road. It was like comparing an ancient wagon trail to a well-traveled four-wheeled drive road.

The road could be hard to travel if It rained or snowed. It was frequented by steep inclines and rocky boulders trying to poke their heads out of the ground. These rocks laid there just waiting to cut tires or even puncture an oil pan. But isn't that what helps make elk hunting trips so exciting and helps you think of Daniel Boone and the old hunting trips for game, so you can put food on the table.

The day we left for hunting the elusive wapiti, it was lightly raining the night before and now was starting to form that white flakes we call snow. Being the aggressive hunters that we were, a little snow falling was not going stop us. Besides you can track the elk better in snow and maybe they will come down lower in the basin to feed. We drove an old rebuilt school bus, (our camper) on highway until we came to the Sunlight Basin turnoff road. We could tell right away that several vehicles were in front of us. The tracks in the light snow covering indicated that more hunters were headed up the mountain. The higher we drove up the mountain, the harder the snow was falling. After a couple miles, we came to a spot where the road started to elevate at a rapid rate. A steep slope awaited us. After trying to make the climb with smooth tires, it was obvious that the tires needed some help. Time to get the tire chains on to help the tires with traction. This was not a fun attempt. The chains did not actually fit the tires. We had to use some bailing wire to custom fit the tires. But whatever works right! After getting the chains on and with standing additional huge amounts of falling snow, we were ready to make the drive up the mountain. Other pickups had passed us and were on their way to set up their hunting camps. It was our turn to get up the mountain.

Slowly, we pulled back into the tracks left by other vehicles and inched our way up the steep incline. We have a problem! The rain the day before had frozen and the snow that was covering the ice was a might slick. We made it another mile up the mountain and then it became obvious that the bus was not liking this trip any more. We pulled over to a widened area and tried flipping coins to see if we wanted to try to go any farther up the road. It was quite dark and getting late. The decision was to spend the night here on the side of the road and see what we could do the next day in the light of day. It was snowing so hard now that we were in a white-out. The windshield wipers were not keeping up with the job assigned to them. We were tired and thought it best to eat a bite and sleep the night away. That sounded good to me.

We did not want to take a chance on carbon-monoxide poisoning, so we turned off the bus and tried to find warm blankets to place over our sleeping bags. Oh, did I say it was snowing? We had a cool night of sleeping. I'm talking about temperature cool here. The morning brought light eventually. However, it was still snowing so hard that the baseball-mitt sized flakes had added up quite plentiful overnight. Over a foot of snow welcomed us to the new day. The chances of us driving up the mountain was slim and none. A good-hearted hunter stopped and offered to pull us up the mountain with his nice large truck. We thought on the idea for a short time. If we did get over the crest of the mountain down in to the basin on the other side, how would we get back up the mountain and out. The horses we had brought, I'm sure would have voted to go home, so did we. It was moved and seconded that we get turned around and head back down the mountain. The hunter with the well-chained vehicle helped get us turned around. That took some creative effort on everyone's part. After some good maneuvering, we were pointing in the right direction and down the mountain we came.

It was true though, my first elk hunting trip was quite an adventure. No elk was had, but a lot of memories were created. The following year we had a successful hunting trip as I did bring home a young bull. One other hunting trip left me with a good memory. I had always heard that one should never just walk up to a downed animal. There were stories of the downed elk or deer jumping out at the hunter and thrusting his antlers through a hunter's leg or torso. In fact, a few years ago, there was a story in our local paper where a fellow did get gored in the leg and bled to death before reaching help. This thought happened to go through my mind as I was approaching a large bull elk that I had shot. For some reason, I stopped about fifteen feet away from the downed elk. He looked dead, but as I took one more step, the elk lunged forward about six feet in my direction. He was right on target. It was a good thing; I had waited to move forward. I shot and put him out of my misery and then I noticed that his antlers were attached at an angle on his head. It made a good picture in the local paper. I'm not sure what had made his antlers sit crooked on his head. Maybe a fight when he was young or just a mishap in his development.

WILD HORSES

Through the years, I have had the pleasure of observing three different herds of wild horses. The Pryor Mountain herd is in northern Wyoming/southern Montana are known quite well. They have been around for a long time. I remember my folks showing me the herd when I was a young boy. They created an interest in me at that time. The horses had a multicolor of browns, blacks, golds, red, and white and seemed very proud of themselves as they showed their running, posing, and jumping skills. I had heard about them from my teachers in grade school. But to see them in person was an awesome experience. The herd can be found on the west side of the Big Horn Canyon National Recreation area northeast of Lovell, Wyoming. It is an interesting area with its Indian teepee rings, buffalo run, cliff paintings, and the ice caves not far away. Lovell has an information station just east of town. A few years ago, I saw the herd again. I've read a lot about the herd in the papers. They capture some of the horse and give them up for adoption. This is to make sure that the herd is kept at a sustainable size for their grazing habitat. The country is a temperate desert and forage is limited. When I last saw the herd, it seemed to have changed very little as they still seemed to be proud of their heritage and freedom to roam the Pryor Mountains. I'm very happy to see and hear that the herd is doing well and are still pretty much isolated from human dependence.

The second herd in Wyoming which I am familiar with is the Green Mountain herd south of Jeffery City, Wyoming. I used to elk hunt that area and I usually saw the herd on the north side of the mountain range. They seemed more spooked by the presence of humans. This is probably due to the mining and hunting that takes place in the area. The horses have a wide variety of habitats to frequent. The higher altitudes of coniferous forest or the Red Desert area on the south side of the mountain to the temperate badland area found on the north side of the mountain. Jeffery City is one of those booms to bust towns that has almost become a ghost town after most of the mining operations have left the areas. I have had the experience of driving through the middle of the herd. The horses looked healthy and their eyes seemed to have a mischievous shine telling me that they were happy sassy. One must see the horses in person to recognize their splendor and witness longevity of adapting to their habitats for so long a time span. I admire their efforts to survive in our modern world, although some humans seem to pester them by negative actions or destroy some of their free reign.

A third smaller herd is found in the McCullough peak region of Park/Big Horn County close to Cody, Wyoming. I was raised not far from this area. I have always tried to get a glimpse of the horses when travelling through the region. Most of the time during the summer months, the horses are easier to see. A couple of smaller water ways exist in the very desolate country. This is not a large herd as the terrain is not very well covered with plants except for along the flood plains of the small creeks that meander through the quite barren region. But as with the other herds, the coloration patterns of the horses are very different. I enjoy knowing that this herd is still doing well as they existed well before my childhood and seem to be continuing their co-existence with the mountain lions and other animals that frequent their domain. To break and train them to ride and be every day cattle horse would be an awesome task if man was to domesticate these horses. Yet, I'm so glad that there are still wild horses that roam our hills and mountains not only in Wyoming, but in other states which have vast uninhabited sections of land for these horses of years ago ancestry to survive and continue to live as the wild horses have for generations.

MOUNTAIN SHEEP

Mountain sheep are found in many locations in Wyoming. In northern Wyoming where I have lived most of my life, I have had the pleasure of several personal experiences with this wonderful species. They are usually quite unafraid of humans invading their habitat or them roaming into human habitat as well.

Many times, over the years as I drive through Wind River Canyon south of Thermopolis, I have seen the mountain sheep along the road, hill side or feeding in one of the two camp grounds. A few times, I have driven my vehicle between the ewes and lambs as they grazed on the green grass. I've walked with in a few feet of them. Of course, most of the times, I forgot to take a camera with me. On a couple occasions I did have my camera and got some good closeup pictures. My favorite pose was of a three-quarter curl ram standing up on a large truck-sized boulder at the base of the hill alongside of the highway. He was overseeing his group of sheep with pride. He looked massive as he was silhouetted against the mountainous background. Of course, I had no camera this time. Now with the camera phones, one usually has instant access to a camera.

Over thirty years ago, the wildlife people introduced a herd of sheep to the Shell-Creek area east of Greybull, Wyoming. The drive from Greybull up through the very small town of Shell and on up to the Big Horn Mountains is one of my favorite travels. It is a very scenic trip including stopping at Shell Falls overlook. In my younger days, my son and I used to walk down in to the canyon far below and cast a line at the fish that were waiting to entertain us. The walk down is bad enough, but the walk back out is going to tax a person's strength and stamina. What we won't do for adventure! Well anyway, I have been looking to see those mountain sheep since the year they put them in the mountains. Finally, a couple years ago, my gold buddy and I were coming back from a good prospecting trip on the Big Horn Mountains and sure enough, the mountain sheep were directly across Shell Creek not more than fifty yards away from the road. Yeah! I finally saw the sheep I had been looking for so many years.

The experience of a life-time happened when I was hunting elk in the Crandal Creek drainage region in the Sunlight Basin area north-west of Cody, Wyoming. We were back into the mountains several miles on horseback. I decided to leave my horse by a small stream and I walked up a well-used trail to the top of a plateau. To my surprise, when I made it to the top, there were about forty or so mountain sheep laying down sunning themselves on the grassy flat area. It was quite a sight. The sheep didn't get excited and run away. In fact, most of them didn't even get up. They looked at me wondering why a human would walk all the way up in to the mountains on a very nice day in October. I was very excited though seeing all these mountain sheep as there were young, ewes and some nice rams present. I walked through the middle of the herd and headed over to the other side of the plateau. I could see a trail heading down the mountain. I wanted to check it out for elk tracks and to see where the trail went. I stopped in the middle of the sheep and looked all around the area. Far across the canyons away from me, I could see a few head of elk. They were way to far away and even if I could get to them, I had better take a knife and fork with me. I would not be able to haul one out very easily. It would take me a life-time to get to them.

I started walking down the narrow trail leading down from the plateau. After I had gone a short distance, I heard something moving ahead of me. I stopped and listened while I waited for what I hoped was an elk coming up the path. About that time, a massive mountain sheep ram came running past me. I'm glad it was past me and not over me. It was close though as I fell to the side of the trail to get out of his way. He was the largest ram I had ever seen. A beautiful or I guess I had better say handsomest ram with his full curl horns. I walked back up on the grassy plateau and the ram was standing there as if he was a statue. A camera, I would have given my lunch for a camera. No such luck! But the incident is locked away in my mind. I will always remember the sight of the mountain sheep herd and how wonderful the scene was to me. It was worth the horse riding, elevated walking and the whole trip to be among the sheep in nature's playground. I did get my small bull elk two days later. But that was anticlimactic after spending the time with the mountain sheep. Besides it was a lot of work getting to the elk and packing it out. It was more fun sitting down in the middle of the sheep and resting and observing them awhile.

SNAKE TALES

It was my sophomore summer in the hay fields. My friend Don and I hauled hay by using a tractor and wagon. My younger brother Dan drove the tractor for us. It was a good way for us to make some good spending money and it also got us in shape for football. We were both good athletes. I'm sure we owed a lot to the hay fields as we started out around seven years old and worked or way up from a driver/unloader to a stacker then to being able to throw the bales up four layers on the wagon. The rancher my dad irrigated for owned five farm-ranches spread out in the norther Big Horn Basin of Wyoming. The haying kept us busy all summer long. We would start around 5 o'clock in the morning and work until 3 or 4 in the afternoon, I had legion baseball practice at five. I was a busy young man.

It was a hot July afternoon when we were out in the field. Don was arranging the bales on the wagon in a pattern that would lock them in, so the bales would hold each other tight on the wagon. A good stacking job would ensure that we did not lose the load on the way out of the field and until we reached the corral where we will unload the wagon and make a hay stack close to the feed bunks. I was throwing the bales up him. The bales weighted around forty-five to sixty-five pounds. It depended on which brand of bailer was being used for the field. Sometimes they used both balers in the same field. This created stacking problems because of the different length of bales. Today the bales were the forty-five-pound size. I was feeling my oats when I picked up a bale and pressed it over my head to throw the bale up three layers high to Don.

Don then started pointing and yelling some muttered remarks. He kept point above my head using some gestures representing panic. I looked up and was looking at a rattlesnake looking me in the eyes. His tongue was trying to reach my nose. For once, I was glad that they used wire to snug up the hay tight in the bales. Evidently the rattle snake was tightly wired close to and could not move. I was so lucky that he was not able to reach my head. He could have struck me right between the eyes. Upon seeing the snake, it did not take me long to throw the bale off to the side. I'm sure Don didn't want to handle it on the wagon. We put the snake into full blown hibernation, then loaded the bale. Then we continued filling our wagon. But only after I took a short sit-down break and a drink of water. I will never forget the look of the rattlesnake staring at me with his tongue flicking out towards my face. The episode has presented many laughs in the telling ever since.

We were between first and second hay cutting. Don, Dan, and I decided it would be fun to go rabbit hunting. Behind my house was a large area known as the badlands. It consisted of many weathered sandstone hills. Between the hills were sagebrush, cactus, yucca, and salt grass. It was good place for rabbits to hang out when they were not eating the hay or beet tops from our fields. Other organisms frequented the region. Along with bobcats, mountain lions, owls, golden eagles, and magpies, there was also an abundant supply of rattle-snakes.

Today, we decided to look at some of the sandstone walls that had names and initials carved into them. Many of the names were familiar to us (including our own). After observing the names and discussing information we knew about the people, we headed to the deep crack between a large sandstone rock formation. Standing above the crack, you could listen to rattlers singing to us as we teased them by dropping small pebbles down into the crack. We did not stay around the rattlesnake den as we did not want them to come out and say hello to us.

We left that spot and headed over towards another loaf-shaped hill. We shot a couple rabbits and sat down for a rest break. We took a drink from or canteen which we brought along. It was in the high eighties or low nineties today. Then I saw a rabbit run up the side of the hill in front of us. I lead the pursuit. The weathered sandstone created natural steps as some of the hillside is more susceptible to weathering then other parts. I started climbing up the side of the hill using the shelf areas as hand holds and foot placements. As I was almost to the crest of the hill, I hear Don yelling and doing his pointing thing. Again, panic was creating some type of foreign language. I could not understand what he was saying so I came back down to see what he was chattering about.

Don informed me he saw a rattlesnake sunning himself on the ledge right above my head. My hand reached right above the snake to the flat space above it. The snake just crawled under my arm into a crack in the hillside. Why it did not strike my wrist or arm is a wonder. I was totally lucky. Right after that happened, my brother came running over to tell me he saw a different rattler crawling on some rocks nearby. We decided it was time to go home for lunch. Not that we were scared by the snakes mind you, we were just hungry.

On another rabbit hunting trip into the badlands, I was walking up between the hills through the sagebrush. I noticed that my shoelace was untied. I bent over and laid the .22-rifle down easily on the ground. Then I reached over and tied my shoelace. Reaching over to pick the rifle up, I was in for a surprise. A small (18") rattlesnake was laying along the gun barrel. The barrel being warm attracted the snake. I noticed the snake was in the process of molting. It looked blind and was not disturbed by my motion. I decided to let the young ratter live another day. I obtained my rifle and left to look elsewhere for more rabbits.

During the summer after I was married, I was working on a ranch northwest of Cody, Wyoming. I was running a large single pivot irrigation system. The irrigation pipe ran down the middle of grass pasture. My job was to adjust the pipes to cover the distance of the small valley. I had to make sure the pipes stayed connected tight so they were not shooting water out. There was a large amount of pressure from the water running through the pipes. Being twenty years old, it was a responsible position to have. I enjoyed the job. The valley created a nice environment to work in. I was studying science in college. I liked to work on farm/ranches. I worked hauling hay and working on a dairy farm during my high school years. The hillsides around the valley were interesting. I could find ancient sea fossils in the limestone formations. Sea stars (vertebrae of ancient plant-like animals) and coral could be found on ant hills or in the rocks nearby.

One day I was down changing pipe position when I saw this baby cottontail rabbit. It must have just come out from its underground home. I thought it would be a nice present to take back to my young wife to raise. I reached down to pick it up. Each time I bent over to pick up the rabbit, it would hop a few steps away. This went on for a while until the rabbit stopped as if it was frozen in place. Ah, this was the time for me to strike. I reached down with both hands and was ready to grab the bunny, Oh my! A large timber rattlesnake was coiled and ready to strike. There was one on each side of me. I quickly did a somersault and rolled forward. When I got up, both snakes were uncoiled and still laying in the spot they were when I had first seen them. I could see a thin board not far away in an old stack yard. With my new found friend in my hands, I returned to find the two snakes coiled again. I won the battle and both sets of rattles became my present to my wife. For some reason, she was not excited to receive them. One set had ten beads and the other had twelve beads. She said I could keep them. Not only could I keep them, but I could keep them out of the house. Later, I looked at my rubber irrigation boots. After careful examination, it looked like both snakes had hit the side of each boot. A few days later, I ran over another large timber rattler that was in the middle of the road. At summer's end, I was ready to head back to college and working on the nearby dairy farm.

"Come on!" I begged my wife, "I want you to go fishing with me."

After several "pretty pleases", I was able to convince my wife to accompany me. I had a small eleven-foot fiberglass boat with a five-horsepower motor. It was nice warm day as we set out for a large lake, to go walleye fishing. We both agree that walleye are the best tasting fish to catch in Wyoming. We travelled the sixty-miles to Boysen Lake, unloaded the boat from the pickup, and made sure all our fishing equipment was in the boat. Our fishing equipment included lifejackets, oars, sound horn, and a first-aid kit.

This lake is well known for the quick arrival of gusty winds. Having this small of a boat, one must stay close to the shorelines. I liked to fish the bays around where we put the boat in. After a couple hours of trolling, we had caught three walleye. This was good for our supper, but not positive for me as we placed a dollar bet on who catches the first fish, the most fish and the biggest fish. I'm zero for three. However, my wife is smiling big time. As Bobbie continues to rub in the details of our bets, I venture a little farther out into the lake.

The water is calm as the sun covers us with its gentle warmth. Then we see it. A snake is swimming towards the boat. Most people don't believe rattlesnakes will swim in water. But in the past I had told my wife about a skier crossing a group of rattlesnakes crossing the lake because of the rising water forcing them out of their den. The skier fell and was bitten so many times that she was killed by the snake toxin. My wife seeing this snake coming towards us, expressed her desire to turn the boat and as they say, "exit stage left!" But as being the person I'm am, I continued to move straight towards the snake. Now the snake looked like it was related to the Loch Ness monster as it swam towards us.

My wife in so many words or less expressed her desire to leave the area. You might say, she is quite afraid of snakes. I wanted to express the fact that if she would forget about the three dollars I owe her; I might move away from the snake. I was not worried about the snake getting into the boat. But the closer the large snake swam towards us, the more emphasis was placed on me by my wife to hastily retreat from the snake. When the snake was a couple feet away, I turned away and we saw the snake continue moving across the lake. We continued to fish as we trolled a little closer to the shoreline.

Looking at the sky in the northwest, we decided that we had better start towards the boat dock. We did not want to get caught out on the water when the wind started blowing. As it turned out, I did have to give my wife the three dollars for the bets. But something made up for my pride deflation. When we got off the lake and were headed home, Bobbie expressed if I wanted her to go fishing with me, I had better get a bigger boat. Oh, what a good idea. By the next summer, I had a sixteen-foot Lund fishing boat. We have enjoyed the boat. We have not witnessed any more snakes crossing the lake. Believe or not, I have even won some of the bets over the years.

TWO AT ONCE

It was a very nice warm summer day as I was fishing at Willow Creek reservoir in southeast Montana. The lake contained an abundance of rainbow and brown trout. I was using a red and silver spinner. It was an enjoyable day I caught and released several small rainbow trout and an occasional German rainbow trout.

During the late afternoon as I kept flipping my spinner out into the lake and reeling it back, a nice hit was made. I proceeded to fight the fish with my light weight pole. When I had the fish to within about twenty feet from the shore, I felt another solid hit. At first, I thought that the fish got hung up on a submerged bush or rock. But then the pumping on the pole became more enhanced and the drag was allowing line to be released. I tightened the drag and began fighting the fish. I took my time reeling and fighting the fish as I did not want to over play it and have it break the line or possibly pull the hook out of its mouth.

After a few minutes, I was able to ease the fish close to shore where I was able to net it. Then instead of one fish in the net, I had two fish. Evidently the three-pound brown trout attacked the small rainbow trout as I was reeling in the smaller fish. I had my friend come over to witness my feat. You know how fishing stories tend to grow. I wanted someone to back me up on this one.

YOU CAUGHT MY FISH

It was a nice warm sunny day of at least 20 degrees out on the iced over lake. It was ice fishing season in northern Wyoming. At least the wind was not howling. The temperature can be cold if the wind behaves itself. I was fishing on upper Sunshine Lake. This is my favorite lake to fish (and many others) in the winter or summer.

The fishing was slow as everyone was waiting for another school of fish to move through the area. It seemed like every fifteen to twenty minutes the poles started fluctuating up and down to show that more fish were in the area. A guy fishing about twenty feet from me had a bite. His pole tip was dancing. I watched as he hustled over to the hole in the ice. The fellow reached down and picked up the pole and gave one of those gigantic heaves as to uncover the water of its ice blanket. Snap went the line and he reeled in a line with no hook or fish.

The three of us watching couldn't resist a little giggling and teasing the fellow about his excitement and his enormous effort at setting the hook. The man took the vocal remarks in a good humorous manner. He was grumbling under his breath as he put another jig on the end of his line. He stated that he had lost his favorite red-haired jig.

A very short time later my pole started giving the bite signal.

The gentleman looked at me and stated, "Sure, you just caught my fish."

We all laughed as we had heard that statement many times before over fishing years. I carefully set the hook on my unsuspecting fish and the fight was on. I could tell the fish was one of the bigger fish in the lake by his efforts to stay away from the opening in the ice. I soon worked the fish to ease his head up through the ice passage way. With a little more effort, the fish was pulled up through the hole in the ice and deposited by my feet.

To my surprise, the fish had a red-tailed jig hooked in the corner of its mouth. Of course, we all started laughing as I did catch the other man's fish. I gave him back his jig, but the twenty-one-inch fish went home with me.

MY WISH

It is my wish and desire that from reading these stories, people will relate to the animals and action that is involved. I would hope that the reader will be stimulated in remembering his or her own involvement with nature and all she has to offer. For those people who have not had the chance to witness Mother Nature first hand, I would challenge you to frequent not only the local parks and zoos, but to travel to the pristine places where nature (flora and fauna) can be seen and enjoyed in person.

I have been fortunate to be raised in northern Wyoming and to teach school in North Dakota and Montana. Those areas have allowed me to live in sparsely populated regions where I was able to observe and be a part of the actions of animals as they lived and competed with one another in Mother Nature land.

What a way to be raised (Tom Sawyer-Daniel Boone). I am pleased to share my nature experiences with the reader. My youth, adolescent, and adult life has allowed me to see and be a part of many special happenings. With my hobbies of fishing and prospecting, I'm sure many more exciting stories will find their way in to my life.